Becoming a Strategic Business Leader.

The Ultimate All-In-One Guide

Created by Adam Niazi, BSc, FCCA, MSc.

ISBN: 978-1-3999-6859-1

A copy of this book is available from the British Library.

Table of Contents

About The Author

Adam Niazi is a qualified professional with a wealth of experience in finance, entrepreneurship, strategic leadership, and education.

Adam holds a BSc in Accounting and Finance, complemented by an MSc in Professional Accountancy. As a Chartered and Certified Accountant, he is a respected Fellow of the Association of Chartered Certified Accountants (FCCA). With his strong academic background, Adam has developed a deep understanding of financial principles and practices.

Beyond his academic achievements, Adam is passionate about helping others succeed. He has extensive experience coaching individuals and teaching exam preparation strategies to help aspiring professionals pass the Association of Chartered Certified Accountants (ACCA) exams and become qualified ACCA members.

Adam's industry experience spans diverse sectors, including investment banking, providing him with valuable insights into financial markets and strategic decision-making. Additionally, he has successfully invested in start-ups and property, showcasing his ability to identify promising opportunities and navigate complex investment landscapes.

Drawing on his entrepreneurial spirit, Adam has also founded and grown his own start-up companies. This first-hand experience has equipped him with a deep understanding of the challenges and rewards of entrepreneurship.

With his combined expertise in finance, entrepreneurship, and education, Adam Niazi is dedicated to sharing his knowledge and empowering individuals to excel in strategic business leadership and financial management.

Introduction

Welcome to an extraordinary journey that will transform you into a master of strategic leadership. If you are an aspiring business professional seeking to enhance strategic acumen, then this book is your key to unlocking unparalleled success.

Do you want to level up your leadership skills? This book offers you an opportunity to tap into the theoretical secrets of successful strategic business leadership and aims to open doors to a world of limitless potential.

Strategic leadership is a coveted skill set in today's dynamic business landscape. Whether you're an entrepreneur, a manager, a director, or an aspiring executive, the principles and practices explored in this book will empower you to steer your organisation towards excellence.

Discover how to unleash your leadership potential, foster an ethical environment, and create value that sets you apart from the competition. Develop the ability to evaluate governance effectiveness, analyse strategic options, and make informed decisions that shape your organisation's destiny. Gain insights into responsible risk management, harness disruptive technologies, and leverage data analytics to drive transformative change.

This book will also illuminate the importance of talent management, resource optimisation, and the application of high-level financial techniques. By immersing yourself in these pages, you'll cultivate the strategic mindset necessary to propel your career to new heights.

So, if you are an aspiring strategic business leader, prepare to embark on a transformative journey. Let this book be your gateway to unlocking the extraordinary leader within you. The knowledge, skills, and wisdom you will gain here will shape your path towards professional excellence and make you a driving force in the realm of strategic business leadership. Embrace the possibilities and prepare to redefine your future.

Part of being a strategic business leader is to be forward looking, embracing new technologies to assist in becoming more efficient. This book does exactly that. I have embraced the growth of remarkably smart artificial intelligence (AI) technologies by using AI to help craft this book. The drawback of using AI is that sometimes inaccuracies can sneak in. With that in mind, the content may contain inadvertent errors or biases inherent to AI.

Now the legal bit; neither the author nor associated parties are liable for any inaccuracies or decisions based on this content. Readers are advised to approach with discretion and cross-check crucial information. The content provided is meant for educational purposes and should not be considered a substitute for professional advice.

Chapter 1 - Strategic Planning

In this section, you'll learn everything about the strategic planning process (a three-stage planning process developed by Johnson, Scholes, and Whittington), the advantages, and the disadvantages. Additionally, we'll discuss strategic drift, the four phases of strategic drift, and how to avoid it.

Strategic Planning

The benefits include improving the organisation's fit with the external or internal environment. Before diving into more details about this area, let's establish a clear understanding. Strategic planning is all about planning for a company's or organisation's strategy, focusing on long-term growth.

Advantages of Strategic Planning

One of the main benefits is the ability to improve the organisation's fit into the environment, both external and internal.

1.   Better use of resources

Conducting strategic planning allows you to best use your scarce resources. Every organisation has limited cash and capital, and it's crucial to make the best use of these resources. Strategic planning also helps ensure the optimal utilisation of these scarce financial resources. Without proper planning, you may end up wasting your resources instead of using them efficiently.

2.   Provides direction

Strategic planning also provides direction for a company, guiding the organisation in making strategic choices. It ensures that goals are met by holding management accountable. For example, if you have an objective in your strategic plan to achieve £100,000 worth of sales in the first quarter of 2024, strategic planning allows you to track progress and hold yourself accountable.

3. Creates competitive advantages

Another benefit of strategic planning is its potential to create a competitive advantage. By conducting thorough analysis and comparing yourself to competitors, you can identify opportunities and strategies that give you an edge in the market.

Strategic planning offers various advantages, including improved fit with the environment, optimal resource utilisation, goal achievement, and the potential for a competitive advantage. It also provides direction and accountability for the organisation. Without strategic planning, organisations may miss opportunities and fail to reach their full potential. Therefore, having a strategic plan is essential for long-term success.

Disadvantages of Strategic Planning

On the flip side, there are some disadvantages of strategic planning. Let's explore these drawbacks in more detail:

1. Time-consuming and Costly

Strategic planning can be a time-consuming process, requiring extensive analysis and decision-making. It involves gathering data, conducting research, and engaging stakeholders, which can consume significant resources. Additionally, implementing the strategies outlined in the plan may require financial investments, adding to the overall cost.

2. Constraints on Flexibility

One limitation of strategic planning is that it may hinder flexibility and adaptability. If you strictly adhere to the strategic plan, you may miss out on potential opportunities that arise outside of the plan. While the plan provides a structured framework, it can sometimes limit the organisation's ability to capitalise on new and innovative ideas that are not aligned with the predetermined strategy.

3. Limited Relevance in Crisis Situations

Strategic planning may become less relevant during crisis situations. Unforeseen events, such as the COVID-19 pandemic, can significantly disrupt the organisation's operations and render the existing strategic plan inadequate. Such crises often require immediate and adaptive responses, making the predefined strategies less effective in addressing the emerging challenges.

4. Potential Bureaucracy

Another drawback of strategic planning is the potential for bureaucracy to develop within the organisation. The strict adherence to the strategic plan may result in excessive red tape and rigid decision-making processes. This can slow down the organisation's responsiveness and hinder the agility needed to navigate rapidly changing business environments.

While strategic planning offers many advantages, it's essential to acknowledge its potential disadvantages. These include the time and cost involved, constraints on flexibility, limited relevance in crisis situations, and the risk of bureaucratic practices. Understanding these drawbacks can help organisations make informed decisions when developing and implementing their strategic plans.

The Strategic Planning Process

The strategic planning process consists of a three-stage planning model developed by Johnson, Scholes, and Whittington. These three individuals have contributed to the formulation of this process.

Stage 1: Strategic Analysis

Strategic analysis involves assessing the external environment to identify opportunities and threats. By using the SWOT framework (Strengths, Weaknesses, Opportunities, and Threats), you can evaluate both internal and external factors. This analysis helps identify the organisation's strengths, weaknesses, opportunities, and threats. Additionally, it allows for stakeholder analysis, understanding key objectives, and assessing the power and interest of different stakeholder groups.

Gap analysis is another component of strategic analysis. It involves analysing the differences between the desired outcome and expected performance. This analysis provides insights into the organisation's current position and the necessary steps to bridge the gap.

Stage 2: Strategic Choice

Once the strategic analysis is complete, the next step is strategic choice. At this stage, you select the strategy that aligns with closing the identified gaps. The strategy chosen should provide a competitive advantage over competitors and foster growth. It involves identifying the markets and products the organisation should focus on. Moreover, the strategic choice considers various approaches, such as organic growth, acquisitions, partnerships, joint ventures, franchising, and more. It is essential to carefully evaluate which strategy is the most suitable for the organisation's needs.

Stage 3: Implementation

Implementation is the execution of the chosen strategy. After analysing and selecting the strategy, it's time to put it into action. Implementation ensures that the chosen strategy is effectively carried out. This stage involves translating the strategy into operational plans, allocating resources, and taking the necessary steps to achieve the strategic objectives.

In summary, the strategic planning process comprises three stages: strategic analysis, strategic choice, and implementation. Strategic analysis focuses on understanding the external environment, conducting SWOT analysis, stakeholder analysis, and gap analysis. Strategic choice involves selecting the most appropriate strategy that aligns with the organisation's goals and offers a competitive advantage. Finally, implementation is the process of executing the chosen strategy and achieving the desired outcomes. By following these stages, organisations can effectively plan and execute their long-term strategies.

Strategic Drift: Understanding the Four Phases

Strategic drift is a process that unfolds in four distinct phases. To visualise this, imagine a graph with the y-axis representing the amount of change needed and the x-axis representing the four phases.

Phase One: Incremental Change
In the first phase of strategic drift, incremental change takes place. Over time, small and steady adjustments are made to advance the organisation's strategy.

Phase Two: Strategic Drift
Phase two introduces strategic drift, where the organisation veers away from its ideal strategy. Progress slows down, and it may feel like reaching a plateau with limited changes occurring.

Phase Three: Flux
In phase three, the organisation enters a state of flux. Despite efforts to change, there is a sense of going in circles without any substantial progress. The strategy remains stagnant, lacking any significant alterations.

Phase Four: Transformational Change or Demise
Phase four presents two potential paths for the organisation. If it implements transformational change—rapid and aggressive adjustments—it can regain momentum and realign with its strategy. However, if the organisation fails to adopt this approach and remains in a state of stagnation, it risks falling into demise. In this scenario, the strategy remains unachieved, and the organisation may face liquidation, closure, or failure.

Avoiding Strategic Drift

Let's explore strategies to prevent or mitigate strategic drift and maintain a positive trajectory towards achieving our goals.

Continuous Assessment of the External Environment
Regularly assess the external environment for potential changes. For instance, during the COVID-19 pandemic, businesses had to adapt to lockdowns and social restrictions by shifting to online platforms. By staying aware of such changes, organisations can swiftly adapt their strategies.

Embracing Flexibility and Agile Systems
Establish flexible systems that enable quick adjustments to changing circumstances. Avoid rigid bureaucratic structures that hinder adaptation and change. A flexible approach allows for agility and responsiveness to new opportunities and challenges.

Fostering a Positive Culture of Change

Cultivate a positive culture within the organisation that embraces change. Encourage employees to see change as an opportunity for growth and improvement rather than a threat. This mindset facilitates the acceptance and implementation of strategic adjustments.

Clear Understanding of Mission and Objectives

Ensure that everyone in the organisation has a clear understanding of the mission and objectives. Without a shared understanding, it becomes challenging to align efforts and make strategic decisions that lead to goal attainment.

Strong Leadership

Strong leaders play a pivotal role in strategy execution. They provide guidance, drive initiatives, and ensure the organisation remains on track. Without strong leadership, strategies lack direction and may falter.

Understanding the four phases of strategic drift and implementing strategies to avoid it is crucial for organisational success. By embracing flexibility, continuous assessment, fostering a positive culture of change, and having clear objectives and strong leadership, organisations can navigate through potential drift and maintain a positive trajectory towards achieving their strategic goals.

In this chapter, we have covered various aspects of strategic planning, including its advantages and disadvantages. We have also explored the strategic planning process, specifically the three-stage planning model developed by Johnson, Scholes, and Whittington. Furthermore, we have discussed strategic drift and its four phases. Finally, we have explored strategies for avoiding strategic drift.

Chapter 2 - Strategic Analysis

This chapter covers several fundamental models and frameworks that will provide an in-depth understanding of various strategic concepts. We will also consider how these can be applied to real-world situations. These models include PESTEL analysis, Five Forces analysis, Porter's Diamond, strategic capabilities, value chain analysis, and SWOT analysis.

PESTEL

PESTEL is an acronym for political, economic, social, technological, environmental, and legal. This framework is useful for analysing the external environment of an organisation.

Political Factors:
Consider not only changes in government or policies but also political stability, government regulations, and potential political unrest. How might these factors influence our organisation's operations, market access, or relationships with stakeholders?

Economic Factors:
In addition to assessing the impact of a recession, think about other economic indicators such as inflation, interest rates, and consumer purchasing power. How might fluctuations in these factors affect our organisation's pricing, sales volume, or overall financial performance? Furthermore, consider global economic trends and their potential ramifications on our industry or market.

Social Factors:
Explore societal trends, cultural norms, and consumer behaviour. How are attitudes and preferences changing? What social issues or movements could impact our organisation's reputation or customer base? Are there any demographic

shifts or lifestyle changes that we should be aware of and respond to?

Technological Factors:
Beyond artificial intelligence and automation, consider other emerging technologies relevant to our industry. Are there new innovations that could disrupt our business model? How can we harness technology to enhance our products, services, or operational efficiency? Additionally, analyse the digital landscape and the influence of social media and online platforms on customer engagement and marketing strategies.

Environmental Factors:
Extend the analysis of the organisation's geographical location and resource usage to include environmental sustainability. Assess the potential impact of climate change, natural disasters, or environmental regulations on our operations, supply chain, or product development. Also, consider consumer demand for environmentally friendly products and the competitive advantage of adopting sustainable practices.

Legal Factors:
Expand the examination of legal factors to include intellectual property rights, labour laws, health and safety regulations, and data protection requirements. How might changes or developments in these areas affect our organisation's operations, compliance obligations, or competitive position? Additionally, consider international trade agreements or political decisions that could influence import/export regulations or market access.

By expanding the analysis of each PESTEL factor, we can gain a more nuanced understanding of the external environment and its potential implications for our organisation's future growth. This comprehensive approach enables us to identify opportunities, anticipate challenges, and make informed strategic decisions.

Five Forces Analysis: Assessing Potential Impacts on Future Margins

The Five Forces Analysis is a key strategy used to analyse the potential impacts on future margins, specifically focusing on price margins. This model consists of five prongs that examine different aspects of the competitive landscape. Let's explore each force in more detail.

Threat of New Entrants:
The presence of new competitors entering the market can pose a threat to existing organisations. This can lead to a reduction in margins as businesses compete to attract customers. For instance, if a new competitor starts selling headphones for £100 while our price was previously £120, we may need to lower our prices to remain competitive. It's important to consider factors such as differentiation and barriers to entry when evaluating the threat of new entrants.

Bargaining Power of Suppliers:
The bargaining power of suppliers can impact margins. If suppliers have greater bargaining power and increase their prices, it can lead to reduced margins for organisations. For example, if our selling price is £100 and the supplier raises their cost from £50 to £70, our margin decreases to 30% from 50%. Analysing supplier relationships and potential alternatives is crucial to managing this force effectively.

Threat of Substitutes:
The presence of substitutes can impact an organisation's future margins. It's essential to identify potential substitutes for the products or services being offered. For instance, advancements in artificial intelligence and automation may render certain roles obsolete. Assessing the availability and viability of substitutes helps determine the potential impact on margins.

Bargaining Power of Buyers:
The bargaining power of buyers, especially if there is a dominant buyer in the market, can influence margins. If a significant buyer accounts for a large portion of sales, they may leverage their position to negotiate lower prices, reducing margins. Evaluating the buyer landscape and diversifying customer base can mitigate risks associated with buyer bargaining power.

Competition and Rivalry:
Existing competition and rivalry can directly impact an organisation's margins. Competitors may engage in price reductions, expansion strategies, or acquisitions to gain a competitive edge. Understanding the competitive landscape, monitoring competitors' actions, and identifying unique value propositions are key to managing this force effectively.

In summary, the Five Forces Analysis helps analyse potential impacts on future margins by considering new entrants, suppliers, buyers, substitutes, competition and rivalry. By thoroughly evaluating each force and understanding their influence on margins, organisations can develop strategies to maintain or enhance their competitive position.

Porter's Diamond: Analysing Potential Foreign Market Expansion

Michael Porter is a renowned economist, researcher, and professor at Harvard Business School. He is widely recognised for his contributions to the field of strategic management, including his framework on competitive strategy.

Porter concluded a framework commonly referred to as Porter's Diamond (1990)[1]. It is used to analyse the potential for

---

[1] *Porter, M. E. (1990). The Competitive Advantage of Nations: The New Paradigm for Company Competitiveness and Global Strategy :*

expanding into new foreign markets. When considering international expansion, there are four main factors to be taken into account.

Factor Conditions:
Factor conditions encompass basic factors like weather and local raw materials, as well as advanced factors such as telecommunications infrastructure and the education system. Understanding the availability and quality of these factors in the target market is crucial for expansion planning.

Related and Supporting Industries:
The presence of world-class suppliers and supporting industries is important for a successful expansion. Evaluating whether the necessary resources and services can be efficiently obtained from local suppliers, aids in determining the viability of entering a particular foreign market.

Firm Structure, Strategy, and Rivalry:
The structure of the organisation, its strategic approach, and the level of rivalry within the foreign jurisdiction play a significant role in expansion decisions. Factors such as ownership, market competitiveness, and the intensity of rivalry need to be carefully evaluated.

Demand Conditions:
Understanding the demand conditions in the foreign market is essential. Assessing whether the target market has demanding customers who will embrace the organisation's products or services is crucial for successful expansion.

To recap, Porter's Diamond model focuses on four main factors: factor conditions, related and supporting industries, firm structure, strategy, rivalry, and demand conditions. By

---

Creating a Competitive National, State of Local Economy. United States: Harvard Business School Management Programs.

considering these factors, organisations can gain insights into the suitability of potential foreign markets for expansion.

Strategic Capabilities: Coping with Changes in the External Environment

The strategic capabilities model helps analyse an organisation's ability to adapt to changes in the external environment. It differs from PESTEL analysis in its approach.

Resources and Competencies:
This model emphasises the importance of resources and competencies. Resources refer to the assets an organisation possesses, including capital and raw materials. Competencies encompass the skills and expertise of the staff and management. Understanding the organisation's resources and competencies is vital for survival and competition in a challenging environment.

Threshold Capabilities:
Threshold capabilities are the minimum requirements for an organisation to function and survive in a competitive environment. These include essential resources and basic competencies that allow the organisation to operate, albeit without significant growth or competitive advantage.

Capabilities for Competitive Advantage:
On the other hand, capabilities for competitive advantage go beyond mere survival. These are unique resources and core competencies that enable an organisation to differentiate itself and excel in the market. Investing in capital, leveraging exceptional raw materials, and employing highly skilled employees are examples of capabilities for competitive advantage.

To summarise, the strategic capabilities model distinguishes between threshold resources and competencies needed for survival, along with the unique resources and core competencies that lead to flourishing and competitive advantage. This framework helps organisations identify their position and potential for growth in the face of external changes.

Value Chain Analysis: Determining Competitive Advantage

Value chain analysis is a model that assists in identifying the source of an organisation's competitive advantage or disadvantage. It comprises five primary operational departments/stages and four supporting activities.

Operational Departments:
The model separates the organisation into nine areas to evaluate advantages, disadvantages, and the source of competitive advantage or disadvantage. These operational areas include:

a. Inbound Logistics: Activities related to receiving, storing, and distributing inputs.
b. Operations: Processes involved in transforming inputs into outputs.
c. Outbound Logistics: Activities involved in storing and delivering the final product or service.
d. Marketing and Sales: Efforts to promote and sell the product or service.
e. Service: Activities related to customer support and after-sales service.

Supporting Activities:
Support activities provide the foundation for the operational departments. The four primary support activities are:

a. Infrastructure: The organisation's overall structure, systems, and resources.

b. Technology: The utilisation of technology to enhance operations and competitiveness.

c. Human Resource Management: Activities related to hiring, training, and developing personnel.

d. Procurement: Processes involved in acquiring necessary inputs for operations.

By examining each of these nine areas, organisations can assess whether they contribute to a competitive advantage or disadvantage. Factors such as cost-effectiveness and quality can be evaluated to determine their impact.

SWOT Analysis: Assessing Strategic Position

SWOT analysis is a widely used model in both small and large enterprises. It combines internal and external analyses to understand an organisation's overall strategic position. The acronym SWOT stands for Strengths, Weaknesses, Opportunities, and Threats.

Strengths and Weaknesses:
Strengths refer to internal factors that give the organisation a competitive edge, such as unique capabilities or resources. Weaknesses are internal factors that hinder the organisation's performance, such as inadequate resources or skills.

Opportunities and Threats:
Opportunities are external factors that the organisation can capitalise on to enhance its position or expand into new markets. Threats are external factors that pose risks or challenges to the organisation's success, such as competition or regulatory changes.

By conducting a SWOT analysis, organisations gain insights into their internal strengths and weaknesses, as well as external opportunities and threats. This analysis helps inform strategic decision-making and identify areas for improvement.

In summary, SWOT analysis is a straightforward yet effective model that examines internal and external factors to assess an organisation's strategic position. By understanding strengths, weaknesses, opportunities, and threats, organisations can make informed decisions and devise strategies for success.

Chapter 3 - Performance Analysis

Performance analysis primarily comprises three key strands: quantitative analysis, benchmarking, and the Baldridge performance excellence.

Quantitative Analysis: Examining Numbers

Quantitative analysis is a fundamental aspect of performance analysis that utilises numerical data to assess an organisation's performance. Financial ratios can include gross profit ratios, liquidity ratios, inventory turnover days, and many others. Familiarising yourself with these key ratios and their application is highly recommended. It is often effective to employ three or four key ratios and provide explanations for any observed changes in any given scenario.

Non-financial Data: Exploring Numerical Insights

Beyond financial data, non-financial numerical information is also available for analysis. This data, although not directly related to financial aspects, still holds quantitative significance. You may encounter non-financial data in table format, requiring interpretation and utilisation. Sometimes, tables supplement the data provided, while other times, the information is presented in a narrative format. It is essential to be well-versed in interpreting both table-based and narrative-based non-financial data.

Benchmarking: Understanding Performance Relative to Peers

Benchmarking is a highly effective tool utilised by organisations, regardless of their size, to assess their performance in comparison to peers and competitors. It serves as a means to identify areas for improvement and analyse the strategies employed to achieve high performance. By implementing benchmarking, organisations can enhance their processes and overall performance. There are three main types of benchmarking: internal benchmarking, competitive benchmarking, and best-in-class benchmarking.

Internal Benchmarking: Comparing Internal Best Practices

Internal benchmarking involves evaluating and understanding the best practices within an organisation by comparing processes in different departments. This form of benchmarking allows for an assessment of performance within the organisation itself.

Competitive Benchmarking: Assessing Performance against Competitors

Competitive benchmarking is the type most commonly associated with the term 'benchmarking'. It entails comparing the performance of one organisation to that of its competitors. For example, it could involve examining the performance of Coca-Cola versus Pepsi or Apple versus Samsung. By evaluating performance in relation to competitors, organisations can gain insights into their relative standing in the market.

Best-in-Class Benchmarking: Learning from Other Industries

Best-in-class benchmarking focuses on analysing the performance of similar processes in different industries. Its purpose is to identify and learn from the best practices employed by top performers, even if they operate in a different industry. This type of benchmarking enables organisations to strive for excellence by adopting effective strategies, regardless of the industry they belong to.

Baldridge Performance Excellence: A Framework for Organisational Improvement

The Baldridge Performance Excellence model is a comprehensive framework that enables organisations to assess their profile in terms of the environment, relationships, and challenges they face. This model consists of seven stages that guide organisations in understanding and improving their performance.

Leadership: The Cornerstone of High Performance
Leadership plays a crucial role in ensuring high performance within an organisation. The first stage of the Baldridge model emphasises the importance of strong and effective leadership. Organisations must assess the performance of their leadership and take appropriate actions to drive positive change.

Strategic Planning: Linking Goals and Actions
Strategic planning is a critical stage that should be closely aligned with the other stages of the Baldridge model. Organisations need to evaluate the effectiveness of their strategic planning process and determine if it provides the necessary information for informed decision-making.

Customer and Market Focus: Delivering Value to Customers
Organisations must assess their treatment of customers, ensuring fairness and customer satisfaction. Evaluating the organisation's market focus, including marketing efforts and target consumers, is essential for identifying areas of improvement.

Measurement, Analysis, and Knowledge Management: Leveraging Information
This stage focuses on measuring and analysing various components of the organisation's processes. Organisations should evaluate financial performance and effectively manage knowledge within the organisation to drive improvement.

Workforce: Assessing Productivity and Turnover
The workforce as a whole, beyond just leadership, plays a vital role in organisational performance. Evaluating the productivity

and turnover rates of employees allows organisations to identify areas where improvements can be made.

Process Management: Streamlining Operations
Efficient processes are crucial for organisational success. Organisations should evaluate their processes to determine if there is excessive red tape or bureaucracy. Simplifying processes and promoting efficiency can enhance performance.

Results: Identifying Weak Spots and Driving Improvement
The final stage of the Baldridge model involves analysing the results of the previous six stages. By assessing the outcomes, organisations can identify areas of weakness and initiate iterative improvements to enhance overall performance.

The Baldridge Performance Excellence model offers a comprehensive framework for organisations to assess and improve their performance. Its seven stages, focusing on leadership, strategic planning, customer and market focus, measurement and analysis, workforce, process management, and results, guide organisations in driving continuous improvement. By leveraging this model, organisations can enhance their performance and achieve excellence.

Performance analysis encompasses three main strands: quantitative analysis, benchmarking, and the Baldridge performance excellence. Quantitative analysis relies on numerical information, including financial ratios, to evaluate an organisation's performance. It is vital to comprehend key ratios and their application in case studies. Additionally, non-financial data in both table and narrative formats play a role in performance analysis and require interpretation. By understanding these strands, you can effectively assess an organisation's performance.

Chapter 4 - Strategic Choice

Strategic choice encompasses; competitive strategies, growth strategies and strategy evaluation.

Competitive Strategies: Understanding the Strategy Clock Model

The Strategy Clock model is a valuable tool for analysing competitive strategies. It represents a step-by-step process that outlines various potential competitive positions a business can adopt. The model takes into account the perceived benefits and price of a product or service.

Mapping Competitive Positions on the Strategy Clock

Visualise the Strategy Clock as a diagram, with the y-axis representing the perceived benefits of the product or service and the x-axis representing the price. Based on these variables, there are eight potential positions where an organisation may be situated.

No frills market position: This position corresponds to a low perceived benefit of the product or service along with a low price.

Hybrid or low-price position: Here, the organisation offers a product or service with low pricing points but high perceived benefits.

Failure position: Organisations that have a product or service with high pricing points, but low perceived benefits are likely to face failure. It is crucial to avoid this quadrant.

Differentiation or focused differentiation: This position represents high prices combined with high perceived benefits.

Organisations in this quadrant can charge premium prices due to the higher value they offer.

Growth Strategies and Evaluation

In addition to competitive strategies, organisations also need to consider growth strategies and strategy evaluation.

Growth Strategies: Identifying Paths for Expansion

Growth strategies focus on expanding the organisation's reach and market share. These strategies include market penetration, market development, product development, and diversification. Each strategy offers different avenues for growth and requires careful consideration.

Strategy Evaluation: Assessing Effectiveness

Strategy evaluation is essential to ensure that chosen strategies are effective and aligned with organisational goals. It involves analysing and reviewing the outcomes and impact of implemented strategies. By evaluating strategy effectiveness, organisations can make informed decisions and refine their approach.

Strategic choice involves selecting competitive strategies and growth strategies while ensuring effective strategy evaluation. The Strategy Clock model aids in identifying competitive positions based on perceived benefits and pricing. Growth strategies enable organisations to expand, while strategy evaluation helps assess the effectiveness of chosen approaches. By understanding and implementing these concepts, organisations can make strategic decisions that drive success.

When it comes to developing a successful competitive strategy, there are two crucial elements to consider: critical success factors and key threats.

Critical Success Factors: Key Elements for Success

Critical success factors are the factors or elements that an organisation must achieve to attain success. They play a vital role in shaping the strategy and ensuring its effectiveness. For example, in the context of a no-frills strategy with low prices and low perceived benefits, the critical success factors include eliminating waste and finding cost-effective alternatives for raw materials. By focusing on cost reduction and waste elimination, the organisation can align itself with this strategy and increase its chances of success.

Key Threats: Identifying Potential Risks

On the other hand, key threats refer to the elements or risks that organisations should be aware of and where possible, actively avoid. For instance, in the context of the 'no frills' strategy, one key threat could be a shift in buyer preferences. If buyers no longer prioritise low prices and are seeking higher perceived benefits, the strategy may face challenges. By identifying such threats, organisations can take proactive measures to mitigate risks and protect their strategy.

Focus Differentiation Strategy: Critical Success Factors and Key Threats

In the focus differentiation strategy, where the organisation offers a high-cost product or service with higher perceived benefits, there are specific critical success factors and key threats to consider.

Critical success factors for this strategy include having market expertise and a unique product offering. Market knowledge allows the organisation to understand customer preferences and tailor its offerings accordingly. Meanwhile, a unique product or service creates a competitive advantage and enhances perceived value. Apple, the smartphone maker, exemplifies this strategy by positioning itself as a high-cost brand with superior perceived benefits, despite not always being a technological first mover.

However, this strategy also faces key threats. A recession can significantly impact the demand for luxury or high-cost items. During economic downturns, consumers may reduce discretionary spending and opt for more affordable alternatives, posing a threat to organisations pursuing a focus differentiation strategy. Additionally, the focus differentiation strategy may target a smaller market size, limiting revenue potential. Moreover, since barriers to entry are relatively low in this market segment, competitors can easily enter and increase prices if they can enhance perceived benefits.

A successful competitive strategy involves considering critical success factors and key threats. Critical success factors are the elements that organisations must achieve for success, while key threats are the risks that organisations should avoid. In a no-frills strategy, cost reduction and waste elimination are critical success factors, while changes in buyer preferences pose a key threat. In a focus differentiation strategy, market expertise and unique offerings are critical success factors, while recession, small market size, and low barriers to entry represent key threats. By understanding and addressing these elements, organisations can develop robust competitive strategies

Growth Strategies: Ansoff Matrix

When it comes to growth strategies, the Ansoff matrix provides a framework for considering different approaches. The matrix consists of four quadrants based on two dimensions: existing products or new products on the x-axis and existing markets or new markets on the y-axis.

Market Penetration: Expanding within Existing Markets

Market penetration refers to introducing a new or improved competitive strategy in an existing market. This strategy is best used when the market is experiencing growth. However, there is a risk that competitors may react and lead to stagnation of growth.

Market Development: Expanding into New Markets

Market development involves targeting a new market segment. Strategic alliances are often used to mitigate risks. However, this growth strategy can strain organisational capabilities and requires a new external analysis, such as a PESTEL analysis.

Product Development: Introducing New or Improved Products

Product development focuses on creating new or improved products within an existing market. There is a risk associated with unknown demand for the new product and potential harm to existing products.

Diversification: Entering New Product and Market Arenas

Diversification occurs when an organisation introduces new products in new markets. It can take different forms such as forward, backward, horizontal, or conglomerate diversification. This strategy presents the challenge of different critical success factors, requiring new external analysis and potentially reducing organisational flexibility.

Strategy Evaluation: Sustainability, Acceptability, and Feasibility

To evaluate a strategy, Johnson, Scholes and Whittington (JSW)[2] proposed three key elements: sustainability, acceptability and feasibility, commonly shortened to SAF.

Sustainability: Consistency and Fit

Sustainability assesses whether the strategy is consistent both externally and internally and whether it aligns well with the environment. It considers how new products fit with existing ones in terms of portfolio analysis, identifies synergies with other business areas, and evaluates timing.

Acceptability: Stakeholder Reaction and Risk

Acceptability examines whether the strategy is aligned to the expectation stakeholders have and whether the associated risks are acceptable. It also considers how stakeholders, including ethical considerations, will react to the strategy.

Feasibility: Resources and Capability

Feasibility focuses on whether the strategy is within the organisation's resources and capabilities. It considers whether the proposed timescale is achievable and whether the critical success factors necessary for implementation are present. If not, additional considerations and adjustments may be needed.

By evaluating a strategy against these three dimensions, organisations can gain insights into its potential for success and make informed decisions about its implementation.

---

[2] *Johnson, G., Scholes, K., & Whittington, R. (2008). Exploring corporate strategy: Text and cases. Pearson education.*

Chapter 5 - Strategic Development

In this chapter, we will discuss how we can develop our strategy using three different approaches. Firstly, we will explore the four options for developing a business strategy and the associated methods. We will explore a framework we can use to analyse a businesses' current product/service portfolio called the BCG matrix[3]. This will be followed by the Ashridge portfolio display[4], which examines the alignment between the parent company and its business units.

Developing Your Strategy: Four Options

Let's begin by exploring the four methods/options for developing a business strategy.

Organic Development
Organic development involves starting from scratch, without any assistance from third parties. It requires building your business from the ground up, which can be a slow and risky approach compared to the other options we'll discuss.

Acquisition
The second option is acquisition, which entails purchasing an existing business or company. This strategy can be executed quickly but is often expensive, as it involves a significant cash outlay.

---

[3] *What is the growth share matrix? (n.d.). BCG Global.*
https://www.bcg.com/about/overview/our-history/growth-share-matrix
[4] *Campbell, A. (2014, August 1). Corporate Strategy: The quest for parenting advantage. Harvard Business Review.*
https://hbr.org/1995/03/corporate-strategy-the-quest-for-parenting-advantage

Partnership

The third option involves forming partnerships, such as joint ventures, strategic alliances, or collaborations with other organisations. Partnering with a third party allows for the sharing of skills, knowledge, and costs. It can also lead to the development of economies of scale. However, partnerships can come with challenges, as differing perspectives and disagreements on strategic and operational matters may arise.

Franchising

Franchising is the fourth option for developing a strategy. This involves granting others the right to use your brand in exchange for a license fee. Consider the example of McDonald's, a highly successful franchise. Individuals approach McDonald's, pay a license fee, and gain the right to use the McDonald's brand. While franchising is generally less costly than acquisition, it does involve relinquishing some control. For instance, if a franchisee engages in misconduct, it can damage the franchisor's reputation and brand.

These are the four options for developing your strategy: organic development, acquisition, partnership, and franchising. Each option carries its own advantages and risks. It is crucial to carefully consider the best approach based on your business goals and resources. In the following sections, we will explore each option in more detail, providing valuable insights and guidance to help you make informed strategic decisions.

Portfolio Analysis and Strategic Decision-Making

Portfolio Analysis refers to the process of evaluating your products and services in terms of their fit within the market. This involves considering market growth, market share, and taking actions to improve their positioning. The BCG matrix is a useful tool for analysing portfolios and determining strategic actions.

Problem Child (High Market Growth, Low Market Share)

A product or service with high market growth but low market share is referred to as a problem child. It has potential, but its current size limits its ability to capitalise on the market. To address this, you can choose to invest heavily to increase market share or consider exiting the product/service altogether.

Star (High Market Growth, High Market Share)

If successful, a problem child can become a star. Stars have achieved high market share and continue to experience high market growth. They require significant reinvestment to defend their market share and sustain growth. While they generate revenue, their cash surplus may be limited due to ongoing investments.

Cash Cow (Low Market Growth, High Market Share)

Over time, stars may transition into cash cows. Cash cows have a stable, high market share but operate in a low-growth market. Although their market growth declines, they maintain a strong position. Cash cows generate substantial cash flow, as there is little threat from competitors in a low-growth market. They provide a reliable source of income.

Dog (Low Market Growth, Low Market Share)

Products or services with both low market growth and low market share are considered dogs. Dogs are not desirable as they are too small to benefit from economies of scale and further investments are not justified. The recommended course of action is to divest and exit these offerings.

Applying Portfolio Analysis to the Public Sector

Portfolio analysis can also be applied to public sector organisations, such as the National Health Service (NHS) in the UK. In this context, the BCG matrix can be adapted by replacing market share and market growth with public need and funding effectiveness versus value for money.

Considering the NHS as an example, the public need for healthcare is high, and funding effectiveness is a critical factor. If a product or service demonstrates low value for money but high public need, strategic decisions must be made. This may involve engaging in public campaigns to educate the public about the necessity of the service or seeking additional funding to address the gap.

Portfolio analysis, using the BCG matrix, allows organisations to evaluate their products and services based on market growth and market share. By identifying problem children, stars, cash cows, and dogs, strategic decisions can be made to optimise the portfolio's performance. The same principles can be applied to the public sector by considering public need, funding effectiveness, and value for money. Effective portfolio analysis enables organisations to allocate resources and make informed decisions to achieve their strategic objectives.

Ashridge Portfolio Display: Examining Strategic Fit

The Ashridge Portfolio Display is a valuable model that assesses the strategic fit between a parent company and its business units. It focuses on the ability to add value to the business unit and the corresponding benefits derived from it. By evaluating the opportunities to add value and comparing them to the ability to do so, this model provides insights into the optimal management approach.

Keeping Business Units Independent

Consider a scenario where a business unit has a low ability to add value. In this case, the unit lacks the necessary skills or knowledge to contribute significantly. However, there exists a high opportunity to add value. In such situations, it is advisable to keep the business unit independent. Allowing the unit to be independently managed and leveraging its expertise enables it to capitalise on the available opportunities. While the parent company may not possess the ability to add value, it recognises the value in letting the unit operate autonomously to maximise its potential.

Understanding the Four Segments

To summarise, let's explore the other three segments of the Ashridge Portfolio Display model:

Alien Territory: Low Opportunity and Low Ability

When a business unit presents low opportunities and low abilities to add value, it falls under the "alien territory" segment. This segment indicates that the unit is not aligned with the strategic goals of the parent company, and therefore, it is advisable to divest from it. Exiting such a segment allows the company to focus its resources on more promising opportunities.

Heartland Segment: High Opportunity and High Ability

In contrast, the Heartland segment represents business units that possess both high opportunities and high abilities to add value. These units are highly desirable, as they align with the strategic goals of the parent company. It is crucial for the company to nurture and invest in these units, leveraging their potential for significant growth and success.

Value Trap: High Ability but Low Opportunity

The value trap segment is characterised by a high ability to add value but a low opportunity to do so. While the business unit has the capability to create value, the limited market or industry conditions restrict its potential. In this scenario, the parent company must carefully evaluate the segment. It may consider various options, such as divesting from the segment, exploring new markets, or repositioning the business unit to leverage untapped opportunities.

In conclusion, the Ashridge Portfolio Display serves as a valuable tool for evaluating the strategic fit between a parent company and its business units. By considering the ability and opportunity to add value, organisations can make informed decisions about the management and development of their portfolio.

In conclusion, the Ashridge Portfolio Display is a valuable tool for evaluating the strategic fit between a parent company and its business units. Alongside the BCG Matrix and other strategic development models, it enables organisations to make informed decisions about their portfolio and optimise their overall strategic direction.

Chapter 6 – Governance and Its Principles

This chapter will discuss the concept of governance, exploring its general principles and various approaches. Our aim is to provide a comprehensive understanding of governance and its implications. Let's begin with an overview of governance, specifically focusing on corporate governance.

Balancing Ownership and Control

Corporate governance involves a continuous debate surrounding the relationship between company ownership and control. This discussion is closely tied to agency theory, which we will explore in detail later. Shareholders, as owners of the company, strive to increase shareholder wealth. On the other hand, directors, who work for the shareholders, hold control over the day-to-day operational activities of the business and often seek to enhance their own remuneration. Consequently, conflicts may arise due to diverging objectives between shareholders and directors.

Internal Responsibilities of Governance

Within an organisation, governance encompasses both internal and external responsibilities. Internal governance is concerned with the decision-making processes of the board of directors, who determine the strategic direction of the company. It also facilitates risk assessment and enables appropriate responses to identified risks. Additionally, internal governance involves the establishment of operational controls to ensure smooth and efficient operations.

External Responsibilities of Governance

On the external front, corporate governance is influenced by two main factors: regulatory frameworks and codes of practice established by governments, and broader social and ethical responsibilities borne by the company. Regulatory frameworks provide a legal framework for governance, while codes of practice serve as guidelines to promote best practices. Moreover, companies are increasingly expected to fulfil social and ethical responsibilities beyond legal obligations. We will discuss each of these aspects in greater detail throughout this chapter.

In this introductory chapter on governance, we have laid the foundation for understanding the principles and elements of governance. We have explored the interplay between ownership and control, as well as the internal and external responsibilities that govern corporate practices. As we progress through this book, we will probe deeper into the intricacies of governance, offering insights and analysis to help navigate the complex landscape of corporate governance.

Key Concepts in Governance

To understand governance fully, it is crucial to grasp the 11 key concepts that underpin it. These concepts serve as guiding principles for effective governance. Memorising and comprehending these concepts will provide a strong foundation for analysing and discussing governance practices. Let's explore these key concepts:

1. Fairness: Ensuring equitable treatment and equal opportunities for all stakeholders.
2. Transparency: Promoting openness and accessibility of information to stakeholders.
3. Honesty: Upholding truthfulness and integrity in all actions and communications.
4. Independence: Maintaining autonomy and impartiality in decision-making processes.
5. Reputation: Safeguarding and enhancing the organisation's standing and credibility.
6. Integrity: Adhering to a strict moral and ethical code.

7. Accountability: Taking responsibility for actions and outcomes.
8. Scepticism: Adopting a questioning attitude and critically assessing evidence.
9. Judgment: Applying informed and balanced decision-making.
10. Responsibility: Fulfilling duties and obligations to stakeholders.
11. Innovation: Encouraging creativity and adapting to changing circumstances.

While most of these concepts are self-explanatory, some students may struggle with certain ones. Let's focus on scepticism, integrity, and accountability:

Scepticism: Scepticism entails consistently questioning and critically evaluating the appropriateness of actions. It involves subjecting evidence to rigorous scrutiny and avoiding complacency.

Integrity: Integrity involves adhering to a stringent moral and ethical code, acting honestly and consistently with principles and values.

Accountability: Accountability ensures that relevant information is provided to stakeholders and encompasses effective risk management practices.

Understanding the Purpose and Scope of Governance

Governance serves distinct purposes and operates in different contexts depending on whether it pertains to the private or public sector.

Private Sector Governance:
In the private sector, corporate governance serves the purpose of monitoring individuals or groups within the company who control the resources owned by the investors (shareholders). It aims to ensure that these parties act in the best interests of shareholders, maximising shareholder value and safeguarding their investments.

Public Sector Governance:
For the public sector, governance encompasses the structures, processes, and behaviours that guide decision-making within governmental bodies and organisations. It focuses on managing public resources and delivering public services effectively, efficiently, and in accordance with public interest.

By understanding and internalising the key concepts of governance, readers will be equipped to analyse and evaluate governance practices effectively. Additionally, grasping the purpose and scope of governance in both the private and public sectors provides a broader perspective on its application and significance. These foundations will be essential as we examine further into the intricacies of governance in the subsequent chapters.

Objectives of Corporate Governance

The primary objective of sound corporate governance is to enhance corporate performance and accountability while creating long-term shareholder value. It is important to remember that the primary objective of any private company is to increase shareholder value. However, when considering governance in the public sector or non-profit organisations, the purpose differs.

Purpose of Governance in the Public Sector and Non-Profit Organisations

In the public sector and non-profit organisations, governance serves the purpose of ensuring value for money. These organisations are appraised or judged based on their ability to achieve value for money, which comprises three elements:

- **Economy**: This element focuses on measuring the inputs required to achieve a certain service or level of service. It assesses the cost-effectiveness of utilising resources.
- **Effectiveness**: Effectiveness measures the output or impact of the service or facilities provided by the organisation. It evaluates the extent to which the organisation fulfils its objectives.
- **Efficiency**: Efficiency considers the relationship between outputs and inputs. It assesses how well the organisation utilises its resources to produce desired outcomes.

Understanding Agency Theory

Agency theory describes the nature of the relationship that arises from the separation between ownership and control within an organisation. In the context of governance, agency theory highlights the different objectives of shareholders (principals) and directors (agents).

Shareholders employ directors to manage the company on their behalf. However, conflicts may arise due to differing objectives. Directors are accountable to the shareholders, and the directors' objective may focus on maximising their own compensation and short-term gains, while shareholders aim for long-term value and increased share value.

Key Concepts of Agency Theory

To comprehend agency theory fully, it is essential to grasp the key concepts associated with it:

- **Agent**: An agent is employed by a principal (shareholder) to carry out tasks on their behalf. The directors serve as agents of the company.

- **Agency**: Agency refers to the relationship between the principal (shareholder) and the agent (directors). It encompasses the delegation of authority and the accountability of the directors to the shareholders.
- **Agency Costs**: Agency costs are incurred by shareholders as they monitor directors due to a lack of trust or good faith. These costs arise from the differing objectives between the agents (directors) and principals (shareholders).
- **Fiduciary Responsibility:** Directors have a fiduciary responsibility, a legal obligation, to act in the best interests of the shareholders. They must prioritise the long-term value and objectives of the shareholders.
- **Objectives**: The objectives of directors may focus on large salaries, high bonuses, and status, whereas the shareholders' objective is wealth maximisation through increased share value and dividend income.

Importance of External Audit and Stakeholder Engagement

One crucial aspect of agency costs is the external audit fee, which helps to monitor and mitigate risks associated with agency conflicts. Additionally, attending meetings, reading annual reports, and analysing analyst reports contribute to effective stakeholder engagement.

Understanding the objectives of corporate governance, as well as the key concepts of agency theory, provides valuable insights into the dynamics of governance and the relationship between shareholders and directors. By comprehending these concepts, stakeholders can navigate the complexities of governance and make informed decisions that align with the organisation's long-term value and objectives.

Shareholder Theory

Shareholder theory suggests that organisations have a responsibility not only to their shareholders but also to a broader range of stakeholders. Stakeholders encompass various groups of people beyond shareholders, although shareholders themselves are often considered stakeholders. These stakeholders can include management, society, customers, suppliers, government, community, future generations, employees, and, of course, shareholders.

Understanding Stakeholder Claims

Stakeholder claims refer to the desires or expectations that stakeholders have from an organisation. Claims can revolve around the influence a stakeholder seeks to exert on the organisation based on how they are affected by its activities. There are two types of claims: direct claims and indirect claims.

- **Direct Claims**: Direct claims are made by stakeholders directly to the organisation, and they tend to be explicit and unambiguous. For instance, trade unions are an example of stakeholders who make direct claims. In the current scenario in the UK, various professions, such as nurses, barristers, ambulance drivers, paramedics, and teachers, have voiced their concerns through strikes.
- **Indirect Claims:** Indirect claims arise when stakeholders do not have a direct voice or representation. Individual customers of large organisations are often considered to have indirect

claims since they may lack the means or platform to voice their concerns effectively. Similarly, concerns regarding environmental impacts can be seen as indirect claims, as the environment itself cannot directly communicate its needs or desires.

The Significance of Stakeholder Engagement

Recognising and addressing stakeholder claims is crucial for organisations to maintain positive relationships and fulfil their broader responsibilities. Engaging with stakeholders enables organisations to understand and consider their perspectives, needs, and expectations. By incorporating stakeholder input into decision-making processes, organisations can foster trust, mitigate risks, and enhance their overall performance.

Shareholder theory emphasises that organisations have responsibilities beyond their shareholders and should consider the interests of various stakeholders. Stakeholder claims represent the expectations stakeholders have from organisations, whether through direct or indirect means. Recognising and engaging with stakeholders is essential for organisations to navigate complex stakeholder relationships and uphold their broader social and ethical responsibilities. By doing so, organisations can work towards achieving sustainable and inclusive outcomes that benefit all stakeholders involved.

Approaches to Governance

When it comes to governance, there are two primary approaches: the rules-based approach and the principles-based approach. These approaches differ in their emphasis and application, and they are prominent in different countries.

Rules-based Approach (United States)

The rules-based approach is commonly observed in the United States. It involves establishing governance codes and regulations that are legally enforceable. Noncompliance with these rules can result in penalties. Under this approach, companies must strictly adhere to the prescribed rules and guidelines.

Principles-based Approach (United Kingdom)

The principles-based approach is prevalent in the United Kingdom. It focuses on adhering to the spirit and intent of the governance code rather than solely following the letter of the law. Companies are expected to comply with the principles, or if they deviate, they must provide explanations in external communications, such as the annual report. Shareholders can then assess the company's governance based on these disclosures, making it a more subjective evaluation compared to the rules-based approach.

Choosing the Appropriate Approach

There are various factors one should consider when determining which approach to corporate governance they should adopt. Considerations include:

1. **Ownership Structure**: If the country has a dominant ownership, such as a family-owned business culture, it may influence the choice of approach.
2. **Legal System**: The characteristics of the legal system in the country play a significant role. The enforceability and effectiveness of the legal framework impact the suitability of a rules-based or principles-based approach.
3. **Economic Conditions**: The state of the country's economy and its economic policies can also affect the choice of governance approach.

4. **Cultural and Historical Factors**: Cultural norms, traditions, and historical context shape the governance landscape. These factors should be taken into account when deciding on the appropriate approach.
5. **Global Economic Outlook and Political Climate**: Consider the broader economic conditions and the political climate to assess how they might influence the governance approach.

Deciding between a rules-based or principles-based approach to governance requires a thorough evaluation of various factors, including ownership structure, legal system, economic conditions, cultural and historical aspects, and the global economic and political outlook. These factors collectively contribute to determining the most suitable approach for a particular country. It is essential to consider these characteristics comprehensively to establish an effective governance framework that aligns with the country's unique circumstances.

Family Structures

Family structures in corporate governance refer to situations where a family holds a controlling number of shares in a company. Let's explore the benefits and disadvantages of such structures.

Benefits of Family Structures

- **Reduced Agency Costs**: Agency costs, which arise from the separation of ownership and control, are minimised when a family directly controls and manages the company.
- **Preserving Family Honour and Ethical Behaviour**: Family-owned companies are more likely to uphold

ethical standards and preserve the family's reputation.

- **Long-Term Decision Making**: Families typically have a long-term perspective and aim to pass the business down to future generations, resulting in strategic decision-making that focuses on sustainable growth.

Disadvantages of Family Structures

- **Limited Knowledge and Expertise:** In cases where the family does not possess a diverse skill set or knowledge base, the company may suffer from limited perspectives and reduced innovation.
- **Potential Family Conflicts**: Family feuds and disagreements can negatively impact the company's operations and decision-making process, leading to conflicts that may undermine its stability.

Insider Dominated Structures

Insider dominated structures are characterised by a small group of shareholders exerting significant influence over a listed company. Typically, pension companies own large stakes in such companies. Let's explore the benefits and problems associated with these structures.

Benefits of Insider Dominated Structures

- **Reduced Agency Problems**: By establishing strong links between owners and managers, insider dominated structures can minimise agency conflicts and improve communication between shareholders and management.
- **Greater Shareholder Influence**: Shareholders in insider dominated structures have greater influence over management decisions, enabling them to align the company's strategies with their interests.

Problems with Insider Dominated Structures

- **Misuse of Power**: Insiders may be reluctant to employ outsiders in influential positions, such as non-executive directors, which can limit diverse perspectives and impede effective governance.
- **Limited Market Influence**: In such structures, the market may have limited power to govern the company. Shareholders may find it challenging to exit their holdings or express discontent, reducing their ability to influence decision-making.
- **Reluctance to Develop Formal Governance Structures**: Insider dominated structures may exhibit resistance to establishing formal governance mechanisms, which can hinder effective oversight and accountability.

Family structures in corporate governance offer benefits such as reduced agency costs, ethical behaviour, and long-term decision-making. However, they can face challenges related to limited knowledge and potential family conflicts. Insider dominated structures, on the other hand, provide benefits like reduced agency problems and increased shareholder influence. However, they may suffer from power misuse, limited market governance, and reluctance to develop formal governance structures. Understanding the dynamics and implications of these governance structures is essential for establishing effective corporate governance practices.

Chapter 7 – Stakeholders

This chapter will explore the importance of corporate social responsibility (CSR) in organisations and what it means to be a 'corporate citizen'.

Defining Social Responsibility

Social responsibility refers to an organisation's consideration and management of its impact on various stakeholders, extending beyond just its shareholders. While some purists argue that corporations are separate legal entities with no responsibilities towards others, CSR recognises the broader societal implications of business actions.

Developing a CSR Strategy

To form a robust CSR strategy, the board of directors must take a firm and public commitment to corporate social responsibility. The following steps are suggested for developing an effective CSR strategy:

1. **Identify Objectives**: The board should clearly define the objectives of the CSR strategy, outlining the desired social and environmental outcomes.
2. **Integration with Business Objectives**: The CSR strategy should be integrated into the overall business objectives of the organisation, aligning it with the company's core competencies and strengths.
3. **Cultural and Governance Integration**: The CSR strategy must be ingrained within the organisational culture, governance framework, and strategic decision-making processes.

Social Responsiveness Strategies

Social responsiveness refers to a corporation's ability to address social pressures and effectively respond to societal challenges. Carol, a renowned expert, has proposed four strategies for social responsiveness:

- **Reaction Strategy**: The corporation denies any responsibility for the social issue in question, completely disregarding its impact.
- **Defence Strategy**: The corporation acknowledges its responsibility but chooses to defend its actions or decisions.
- **Accommodation Strategy**: The corporation accepts responsibility and takes the necessary steps demanded by the situation to address the social issue.
- **Proactivity Strategy**: The corporation proactively surpasses industry norms and adopts a best-in-class approach to social responsibility, going beyond what is expected.

Stakeholders play a vital role in an organisation's success, and corporate social responsibility is an essential aspect of effective governance. Recognising the impact of business actions on various stakeholders and adopting a comprehensive CSR strategy can contribute to the long-term sustainability and positive societal impact of the organisation. Understanding different social responsiveness strategies enables corporations to navigate challenging situations while maintaining a responsible and ethical approach.

Understanding Stakeholder Claims

As previously mentioned, Stakeholder claims refer to the demands made by stakeholders on an organisation. To effectively manage stakeholder relations, Mendelow A.

(1991)[5] introduced a mapping matrix that classifies stakeholders based on their power and interest in the organisation. This matrix, consisting of four quadrants, provides guidance on appropriate actions depending on the stakeholder's placement within it.

Managing Stakeholder Relations with Mendelow's Matrix

Mendelow's matrix serves as a valuable tool for managing stakeholder relations:

- **Key Players**: Stakeholders with high levels of both interest and power fall into this category. Organisations should focus on keeping them satisfied to ensure they do not become influential and potentially disrupt operations.
- **Keep Satisfied**: Stakeholders with low levels of interest but significant power require attention to maintain their satisfaction. Although they may not actively engage, their influence can significantly impact the organisation.
- **Minimal Effort**: Stakeholders with low levels of both interest and power do not demand significant attention. Organisations can allocate minimal effort in managing their relationship.
- **Keep Informed**: Stakeholders with low power but high interest should be kept informed. Regular communication helps maintain their engagement and prevents them from becoming disengaged or discontented.

---

[5] Mendelow, A. L. (1991) 'Environmental Scanning: The Impact of the Stakeholder Concept'. Proceedings From the Second International Conference on Information Systems 407-418. Cambridge, MA.

Corporate citizenship expands the notion of a corporation's role in society beyond its relationship with shareholders. It entails acknowledging accountability and assuming responsibility for the consequences of organisational actions.

Reasons for Embracing Corporate Citizenship

There are compelling reasons for organisations to embrace corporate citizenship:

1. **Government Failure**: In instances of slow legislative action, corporations can act as proactive corporate citizens, addressing social issues before government intervention. This approach ensures the safety of products and services and demonstrates a commitment to societal well-being.
2. **Corporate Power**: Companies that establish themselves as corporate citizens gain influence and wield significant power. By actively contributing to society and shaping lives, they build a positive reputation and attract support from stakeholders.

Stakeholder theory emphasises the need to consider the impact of organisational actions on various stakeholders. Mendelow's matrix aids in managing stakeholder relations effectively, enabling organisations to prioritise efforts and meet stakeholder expectations. Embracing corporate citizenship expands an organisation's role beyond shareholder interests, encouraging responsibility and proactive engagement with broader societal issues.

Chapter 8 – Leadership

This chapter outlines what it means to have effective leadership, highlighting its nature, importance, and key characteristics. We will explore the distinctions between leadership and management, the role of leadership in shaping organisational culture, and the differentiation between entrepreneurship and intrapreneurship.

Understanding the Nature and Importance of Leadership

Leadership encompasses various definitions, but at its core, it involves the exercise of influence over others. A leader is someone who employs interpersonal influence to guide individuals or teams toward the achievement of specific goals. Three crucial elements underpin the definition of leadership: interpersonal influence, multiple individuals to lead or influence, and a shared goal to strive for.

Exploring the Relationship between Leadership and Management

Leadership and management are often used interchangeably, but they represent distinct aspects of organisational dynamics. While management involves the administration of tasks and resources to achieve established objectives, leadership focuses on inspiring and guiding individuals to exceed expectations, fostering innovation and growth.

The Role of Leadership in Shaping Organisational Culture

Leadership plays a pivotal role in shaping organisational culture—the shared values, beliefs, and behaviours that define a company's character. Effective leaders establish and uphold a positive culture by embodying desired values, fostering open communication, and promoting collaboration and trust among team members. By setting an example, leaders influence the overall work environment and employee morale.

Differentiating Entrepreneurship and Intrapreneurship

Entrepreneurship and intrapreneurship are two distinct approaches to innovation and business development. Entrepreneurship refers to the creation of new ventures, often involving the identification of market opportunities and assuming associated risks. In contrast, intrapreneurship involves cultivating an entrepreneurial spirit within an existing organisation, empowering employees to innovate, take risks, and drive internal growth and improvement.

Effective leadership is essential for achieving organisational success. Leaders exert interpersonal influence to guide individuals or teams toward shared goals, contributing to the development of a positive organisational culture. Recognising the distinctions between leadership and management helps to optimise both aspects within an organisation. Furthermore, understanding the nuances of entrepreneurship and intrapreneurship enables leaders to foster innovation and adaptability. By honing effective leadership skills, individuals can inspire and empower others to reach their full potential, driving organisational growth and prosperity.

Understanding Effective Leadership

Trait Theories and Behavioural Styles

When it comes to identifying what makes a leader effective, two prominent approaches are trait theories and behavioural or style theories. Trait theories suggest that great leaders possess certain physical and personality traits that contribute to their effectiveness. However, it's important to recognise that leadership is not solely determined by these traits, as there are exceptions and counterarguments to consider.

Physical Traits and Stereotypes

Trait theories often associate physical attributes like drive, energy, appearance, and even height with effective leadership. While these characteristics are often considered advantageous, it is crucial to acknowledge that effective leaders come in various forms. That being said, we all know a successful leader who may not fit this stereotypical traditional expectation.

Personality Traits and Social Skills

Another aspect examined by trait theories is personality traits. Effective leaders are often described as adaptable, enthusiastic, and self-confident. Additionally, leaders display social traits such as cooperation, courtesy, and strong administrative abilities. These traits contribute to their ability to motivate and guide others towards shared goals.

Limitations of Trait Theory

It is essential to recognise the limitations of trait theory when assessing effective leadership. Counterarguments arise when considering individuals who do not possess the typical physical or personality traits associated with effective leadership. We encounter successful leaders who may be shorter in stature or exhibit behaviours that deviate from traditional expectations, yet still achieve remarkable results.

The Importance of Context and Adaptability

Leadership effectiveness is influenced by various factors, including the specific context in which leadership is exercised. Effective leaders possess the ability to adapt their behaviours and styles to different situations and challenges. They understand the importance of flexibility, empathy, and the capacity to inspire and influence others based on the needs of the moment.

Behavioural Style Theory: An Alternative Approach

The second approach in understanding effective leadership is the behavioural style theory. This theory focuses on different management styles and their impact on leadership effectiveness. Four main management styles are commonly identified: autocratic, democratic, persuasive, and participative. Each style reflects a distinct approach to decision-making and team involvement.

Autocratic Style: The Manager as the Sole Decision-Maker

In the autocratic style, the manager assumes full control over decision-making, expecting obedience without question. While traditionally considered the least effective style, there are instances where autocratic leaders have achieved remarkable success. For example, Steve Jobs, the late founder of Apple, was known for his autocratic leadership, driving the company to become the world's largest technology company.

Democratic Style: Collaborative Decision-Making

The democratic style involves leaders and team members making decisions collectively, based on consensus. This approach emphasises participation and shared decision-making, fostering a sense of ownership and engagement among team members.

Persuasive Style: Influencing Decision-Making

In the persuasive style, the manager retains the authority to make all decisions but believes in motivating team members to accept and carry them out effectively. This style relies on the manager's ability to influence and persuade employees, ensuring their commitment to daily activities.

Participative Style: Considering Team Input

The participative style involves managers consulting with their teams and taking their views into account before making a decision. While team input is valued, the ultimate decision rests with the manager. This style emphasises collaboration and valuing the insights of team members.

The Limitations of Behavioural Style Theory

One challenge of behavioural style theory is that no single style can be deemed universally effective or ineffective. Successful leaders can exhibit a range of styles, and the effectiveness of a particular style often depends on the context, organisational culture, and individual preferences. Therefore, a combination of behavioural and trait theories is often considered essential in understanding and developing effective leadership.

Differentiating Leadership from Management

Understanding the distinction between leadership and management is crucial. While managers focus on setting and achieving organisational goals through planning, organising, directing, and controlling, leaders also prioritise the interpersonal elements of their role. Leaders are willingly followed and listened to by their employees, whereas employees may follow managers out of obligation rather than genuine willingness. Leadership goes beyond authority; it is about inspiring, guiding, and influencing others towards shared goals.

The Role of Leadership in Shaping Organisational Culture

Leadership plays a vital role in shaping organisational culture. Two primary types of leadership are often discussed in relation to culture: transactional and transformational leadership.

Transactional leaders tend to maintain a more passive relationship with their followers, viewing it as a trade-based interaction focused on fulfilling predetermined tasks. In contrast, transformational leaders inspire and motivate their followers, often driving significant cultural shifts and guiding organisations towards new directions.

The Power of Transformational Leadership

Transformational leaders are known for their ability to instigate change and inspire others. They have a profound impact on organisational culture, often driving innovation, fostering a sense of purpose, and encouraging continuous growth. By motivating and aligning their teams towards a shared vision, transformational leaders are instrumental in transforming the culture and driving organisational success.

Entrepreneurship versus Intrapreneurship

Lastly, it is essential to distinguish between entrepreneurship and intrapreneurship. Entrepreneurship refers to individuals who start and own their businesses, taking on the associated risks and financial responsibilities. In contrast, intrapreneurship involves employees who contribute entrepreneurial ideas and initiatives within an existing organisation. Intrapreneurs typically do not possess ownership stakes and face minimal risk of financial loss.

Summary: Incorporating a Holistic Perspective

In summary, effective leadership is a dynamic interplay between various factors, including behavioural styles, traits, situational context, and the ability to inspire and motivate others. While the behavioural style theory highlights different approaches to decision-making and team involvement, it is crucial to recognise that leadership effectiveness cannot be solely determined by a specific style.

Leadership is distinct from management as it encompasses the interpersonal aspects of building relationships, fostering trust, and eliciting voluntary followership. A leader's ability to connect with and inspire their team members is a key differentiator that sets them apart from traditional managers. By cultivating a sense of willingness among employees to follow their lead, leaders can create a more engaged and motivated workforce.

Furthermore, leadership's influence extends beyond day-to-day operations. Leaders shape organisational culture, driving the transformational changes needed for long-term success. Transformational leaders, in particular, have the power to inspire individuals to exceed their own expectations, challenge the status quo, and embrace innovation. Their ability to communicate a compelling vision and create a sense of purpose within the organisation is instrumental in driving cultural shifts and achieving strategic goals.

While behavioural theories provide insights into leadership styles, it is important to recognise that effective leadership requires a holistic perspective. Trait theories, which focus on individual characteristics and qualities, complement behavioural approaches by acknowledging that leaders possess unique traits such as adaptability, enthusiasm, and self-confidence. A comprehensive understanding of leadership combines both behavioural and trait theories to identify the diverse range of skills and attributes that contribute to effective leadership.

Lastly, distinguishing between entrepreneurship and intrapreneurship highlights the different contexts in which leadership can be demonstrated. Entrepreneurs take on the risks and responsibilities of starting and owning their businesses, while intrapreneurs leverage their entrepreneurial spirit within existing organisations. Both roles require leadership qualities, such as innovation, risk-taking, and the ability to drive change, albeit in different contexts.

In conclusion, effective leadership encompasses a multifaceted approach that integrates behavioural styles, traits, and contextual factors. It goes beyond management by focusing on interpersonal relationships, inspiring others, and shaping organisational culture. A comprehensive understanding of leadership acknowledges the diverse range of skills, styles, and contexts in which leadership can be exercised, ultimately paving the way for impactful and transformational leadership.

Chapter 9 - Board of Directors

This chapter focuses on the board of directors, a substantial topic that we will try to condense for better understanding.

The board of directors has several key roles and responsibilities. They provide entrepreneurial leadership and represent the company's views. They decide on a formal schedule of matters for the board's decisions and determine the company's mission and purpose. Furthermore, they select and appoint the CEO, chairman, and other board members, and establish the company's values and standards. The board is also responsible for establishing appropriate internal controls, ensuring the availability of financial and human resources to achieve the company's objectives, and meeting its obligations to shareholders and stakeholders. Their ultimate aim is to discharge their duties effectively.

Listed Companies

For listed companies, which refers to those publicly traded on the stock exchange, certain additional requirements must be fulfilled. These companies must appoint appropriate non-executive directors, also known as NED's. The role and significance of NED's will be explained shortly. Listed companies are also required to establish a remuneration committee, nominations committee, and audit committee. Additionally, they need to assess their own performance and report to shareholders annually. Furthermore, they must undergo re-election at regular intervals.

Re-election for UK Companies in the FTSE 350

If a UK company is part of the FTSE 350, which comprises the largest 350 companies in the United Kingdom, they should present themselves for re-election every year.

Non-Executive Directors

NED's have four primary roles and responsibilities. They contribute to the strategic success of the company by challenging the strategy, offering advice, and scrutinising the decisions and results achieved by the executive directors. They also have a risk role, where they assess the adequacy of internal control systems and oversee the appointment of executive directors' remuneration.

Advantages and Disadvantages of NED's

There are several advantages to having NED's on the board, including their multiple monitoring role, additional expertise, enhanced perception of the company, better communication with stakeholders, and discipline in achieving the company's strategy. As for disadvantages, the main concerns are the potential for increased costs due to a larger board and the need to ensure that the non-executive directors add value and actively contribute, rather than simply being additional members.

The Chairman and CEO Distinction

It is crucial to have a clear division of responsibilities between the Chairman and the CEO (Chief Executive Officer) at the top of the company. No individual should have unrestricted decision-making power. The Chairman is responsible for ensuring that the board effectively sets and implements the company's direction and strategy, while also representing the company's aims and policies to shareholders. The CEO takes responsibility for the overall performance of the company and reports to the Chairman and the Board of Directors.

Reasons for Separating Chairman and CEO Roles

There are several reasons for having separate Chairman and CEO roles. Firstly, the Chairman solely represents the shareholders and avoids any conflicts of interest related to running the company. The Chairman also provides accountability for the CEO and the management team, reducing the temptation to act in self-interest rather than in the interest of the shareholders.

Reasons Against Splitting the Roles

On the other hand, having two high-powered individuals can lead to clashes. Additionally, having a single person making all the decisions can result in less bureaucracy and faster decision-making processes.

Board Committees

Board committees play a crucial role in the functioning of the board of directors, offering numerous benefits and importance. The establishment of committees helps reduce the workload of the board, allowing them to focus on other critical issues. It creates structure within the board's operations and facilitates better communication with shareholders, among other advantages.

Nominations Committee

The nominations committee holds the responsibility of hiring and firing board members. Their key tasks include regularly reviewing the company's structure and size to ensure effectiveness. They make recommendations to the board regarding the balance of executives and non-executives, promote diversity within the board composition, and establish an appropriate balance of power between the Chairman and CEO. The committee identifies and nominates candidates to fill board vacancies and provides recommendations for the reappointment of directors. Importantly, they operate independently for the benefit of shareholders.

Remuneration Committee

The remuneration committee is responsible for determining the pay of the board of directors and senior management. Their primary focus is to establish an appropriate reward policy that attracts, retains, and motivates directors to achieve the long-term interests of shareholders. The committee sets the remuneration of executive directors and the Chairman, ensuring it aligns with performance objectives. They also ensure that remuneration decisions are made objectively, free from undue pressure, and correctly disclosed in the reporting. Additionally, the committee reviews the company's remuneration policy and determines the terms, conditions, and deployment of remuneration for other team members. They design targets and bonus schemes, monitor the structure of remuneration for senior managers, and establish pension policies.

Components of a Director's Remuneration Package

To ensure directors are motivated for the long-term interest of shareholders and increased shareholder wealth, a director's remuneration package should consist of four main elements:

Basic Salary: The basic salary is determined based on the skills required for the role and the individual's performance at the market rate.

Performance-Related Pay: This element of remuneration is tied to the achievement of specific performance measurement criteria. It can take the form of bonuses, share options, and other incentives.

Pension: The pension component should only be calculated based on the basic salary and not include bonuses or benefits in kind.

Benefits in Kind: These refer to non-wage compensations, such as a company car, provided in addition to the regular salary and wages.

Considerations for Director Remuneration

It is important to consider market rates and benchmarking when determining the elements of a director's remuneration package. Performance-related pay should be linked to the company's performance and its long-term goals. For non-executive directors, remuneration typically consists of a basic salary and may include share awards. Equity-based remuneration should be fully vested on the grant date but subject to applicable holding periods, such as a restriction on selling shares within a specified timeframe (e.g., two years). This promotes the long-term interests of the company and aligns with performance measures.

It's worth noting that non-executive remuneration packages generally do not include performance-related bonuses.

Chapter 10 – Reporting

This chapter explores the crucial aspects of reporting to stakeholders, with a particular focus on institutional investors. It discusses sustainability reporting, social and environmental reporting, integrated reporting, and examines the benefits and drawbacks associated with social and environmental reporting. Additionally, it provides insights into the preparation of integrated reports and touches upon the concepts of value creation and the reporting process.

Institutional Investors

Institutional investors encompass various entities, including pension companies and private equity firms. However, the composition of institutional investors can vary widely. The most common types of institutional investors include pension companies, life insurance companies, unit trusts, and investment trusts. These entities manage funds on behalf of individuals.

Institutional Shareholder Intervention

Institutional shareholder intervention refers to situations where it is appropriate for institutional investors to intervene in an organisation. These are the eight conditions that may warrant such intervention:

1. **Strategy**: Institutional investors may intervene if they disagree with the products sold or the markets being serviced by the organisation. They would question whether the company's current strategy aligns with the desired direction.

2. **Operational Performance**: If the company's operational performance is persistently below expectations, institutional investors may view it as a reason to intervene. They would seek improvements to enhance overall performance.

3. **Acquisitions**: Institutional investors may intervene if they disagree with or support the company's decisions regarding acquisitions. Their focus would be on ensuring that the acquisitions align with the organisation's strategic objectives.

4. **Disposals**: Similar to acquisitions, institutional investors may intervene if they have concerns or express agreement with the company's decisions to sell subsidiaries or assets. They would assess whether such disposals align with the organisation's long-term goals.

5. **Remuneration**: Institutional investors may take action if they believe the compensation of directors is inappropriate. They would evaluate whether the remuneration packages are reasonable and aligned with the performance and responsibilities of the directors.

6. **Internal Controls**: Failures in areas such as health and safety, quality budgets, project management, or financial controls may prompt intervention from institutional investors. They would seek to address deficiencies and ensure proper governance.

7. **Succession Planning**: If there is a lack of appropriate planning for executive replacements, institutional investors may intervene. They would emphasise the importance of smooth transitions and the continuity of leadership.

8. **Social Responsibility**: Institutional investors may intervene if the company fails to adequately protect or respond to environmental conservation efforts or other areas of public concern. They would evaluate

the company's commitment to social responsibility and sustainability.

While it is not necessary to memorise each condition extensively, it is important to acknowledge their relevance to institutional shareholder intervention.

Reporting to stakeholders, particularly institutional investors, plays a vital role in ensuring transparency and accountability. Institutional shareholders may find it necessary to intervene in an organisation under specific circumstances, including misalignment in strategy, poor operational performance, contentious acquisitions or disposals, inappropriate remuneration, flawed internal controls, insufficient succession planning, or inadequate attention to social responsibility. By addressing these concerns, companies can build trust, establish effective engagement with stakeholders, and ensure the long-term sustainability of their operations.

Disclosures: General Principles

Disclosures play a vital role in communication between a company and third parties. They involve conveying specific information to shareholders and other stakeholders. One important disclosure opportunity is the Annual General Meeting (AGM), where directors can communicate directly with shareholders. The AGM is the only legally required disclosure to shareholders, and the annual report and accounts often serve as the primary source of information for shareholders. Establishing and maintaining effective communication channels with shareholders and stakeholders is crucial. Disclosure acts as a mechanism to provide transparency and enhance governance.

The Cadbury Report and Transparency

The Cadbury Report was commissioned in response to a series of high-profile corporate scandals in the United Kingdom during the late 1980s and early 1990s. These scandals, such as the collapse of Polly Peck International and the Maxwell Communications Corporation, exposed significant deficiencies in corporate governance and financial reporting practices.

The Cadbury Report, named after Sir Adrian Cadbury, summarised the importance of transparency and information flow in markets. Published in 1992, it emphasised two key findings. Firstly, "the lifeblood of a market is information, and any barrier to that information represents imperfection." This statement highlights the significance of accessible and transparent information for the proper functioning of markets. Secondly, "the more transparent a company's activities are, the more accurately securities shares can be valued." Transparency enables investors to make informed decisions and accurately assess the value and risks associated with a company's shares.

Sustainable Development
Sustainable development involves meeting present needs without compromising the ability of future generations to meet their own needs. An example of unsustainable development is the finite nature of fossil fuels. If we rely solely on non-renewable energy sources without developing renewable energy alternatives, future generations may face energy scarcity. Sustainable development, on the other hand, focuses on practices that ensure the best outcomes for both human and natural environments, both now and in the future.

Environmental Footprint
Assessing a company's environmental footprint involves evaluating its impact on the environment in three primary aspects. Firstly, resource consumption, which measures the company's use of resources such as water, energy, and raw materials. Secondly, harm to the environment caused by pollution emissions. This includes evaluating the negative impact of the company's activities on air, water, and soil quality. Finally, the measurement of resource consumption

and pollution emissions in terms of their qualitative or quantitative harm, or replacement terms.

Disclosures are essential for effective communication between companies and stakeholders. The Cadbury Report highlighted the importance of transparency and information flow in markets, emphasising the need for accessible and accurate information. Sustainable development aims to meet present needs while ensuring a sustainable future for generations to come. Evaluating a company's environmental footprint involves assessing its resource consumption and the harm caused by pollution emissions. By considering these factors, companies can work towards minimising their environmental impact and contributing to a more sustainable world.

Social Footprint: Evaluating Sustainability

The social footprint evaluates sustainability across three areas of capital: human capital, social capital, and constructed capital.

1. **Human capital** refers to the personal health, knowledge, skills, and experience held by individuals, enabling them to effectively take action.
2. **Social capital** represents the network of people and their collective knowledge, which enables them to take action effectively.
3. **Constructed capital** encompasses the material resources, tools, infrastructure, and utilities that individuals produce and utilise to take effective action. By considering these three areas of capital, organisations can assess their social footprint and its impact on sustainability.

Sustainability Audits: Assessing Performance

To gain insights into their sustainability performance, companies can conduct sustainability audits. A sustainability audit involves a comprehensive examination of the organisation's environmental management system and associated arrangements. The purpose is to evaluate the social performance, environmental impact, and overall sustainability practices of the company. By conducting these audits, organisations can gain a deeper understanding of their commitment to social and environmental responsibility and identify areas for improvement.

Social and Environmental Reporting: Benefits and Drawbacks

Social and environmental reporting involves the disclosure of information related to social and environmental issues. Environmental reporting focuses on aspects such as emissions, waste, and energy consumption, providing transparency on the company's environmental performance. Social reporting varies across industries but commonly covers topics such as human rights, employee issues, occupational health and safety, fair pay, and equity.

Benefits of Social and Environmental Reporting

The benefits of social and environmental reporting are numerous. It increases investor interest, enhances the reputation of the company, enables employees to make informed choices about their workplace, and influences consumer buying decisions. Social and environmental reporting can positively impact a company's share price and promote good corporate governance.

Drawbacks of Social and Environmental Reporting

However, there are drawbacks to consider, including the potential for timeliness challenges, high costs associated with reporting, and ambiguity in measuring social and environmental impacts.

Integrated Reporting: Linking Strategy, Governance, and Performance

Integrated reporting establishes the connections between an organisation's strategy, governance, financial performance, and the social, environmental, and economic contexts in which it operates. It highlights the interdependencies and influences between strategy, governance, financial performance, and the broader social and environmental factors. Integrated reporting enables businesses to make more informed and sustainable decisions by considering the broader impact of their actions. It also helps investors and other stakeholders gain a holistic understanding of the organisation's performance and prospects. Integrated reporting is not limited to a separate report but should be integrated within the annual report or equivalent documentation.

The primary objectives of integrated reporting are to improve the quality of information provided to financial capital, streamline and integrate corporate reporting processes, enhance accountability and stewardship, and support integrated thinking in decision-making and actions across short, medium, and long-term horizons. By adopting integrated reporting, organisations can effectively communicate their strategies, governance practices, performance, and prospects within the context of the external environment. This approach promotes value creation and sustainability over time.

The concepts of social footprint, sustainability audits, social and environmental reporting, and integrated reporting underscore the importance of comprehensive and transparent corporate reporting. By evaluating social and environmental impacts, conducting sustainability audits, and adopting integrated reporting practices, organisations can enhance their understanding of sustainability, promote responsible practices, and create long-term value for stakeholders.

Embracing these principles fosters a more sustainable and resilient business environment.

Preparing an Integrated Report: Six Guiding Principles

1. Strategic Focus and Future Orientation

The first guiding principle for preparing an integrated report is to have a strategic focus and future orientation. This involves highlighting significant risks, examining the market position, and understanding the business model. By providing a management view of the organisation's short, medium, and long-term prospects, this principle sets the foundation for a forward-thinking approach.

2. Connectivity of Information

The second principle emphasises the importance of presenting a holistic picture of the company. It involves demonstrating the interrelatedness and dependencies between various factors that impact the organisation. By showcasing the connectivity of information, the report illustrates how these factors influence the company's ability to create value over time.

3. Stakeholder Relationships

The third principle focuses on establishing clear and transparent stakeholder relationships. It recognises the significance of engaging with stakeholders and understanding their interests, needs, and concerns. By addressing stakeholder relationships, the report enables a comprehensive understanding of the organisation's interactions with its various stakeholders.

4. Materiality

The fourth principle is materiality, which involves identifying and disclosing matters that have the potential to affect the value creation of the organisation. Materiality helps prioritise information and ensures that the report includes relevant and meaningful content. By considering materiality, the report provides a concise and focused view of the organisation's key issues and impacts.

5. Consciousness

The fifth principle, consciousness, aims to provide sufficient context for understanding the organisation's strategy, governance, and prospects. It highlights the need to present information in a clear and concise manner, avoiding unnecessary details that may burden the reader. Consciousness ensures that the report provides the necessary information without overwhelming the reader with irrelevant or extraneous data.

6. Reliability and Completeness

The sixth principle emphasises the importance of ensuring the reliability and completeness of material matters. This involves presenting information in a balanced manner, addressing both positive and negative aspects of the organisation's performance. By maintaining reliability and completeness, the report establishes credibility and trustworthiness, enhancing its value as a reliable source of information.

The six guiding principles for preparing an integrated report are strategic focus and future orientation, connectivity of information, stakeholder relationships, materiality, consciousness, and reliability and completeness. By adhering to these principles, organisations can create a comprehensive and insightful report that effectively communicates their strategy, governance, performance, and prospects to stakeholders

Value Creation

The Value Equation

In the context of value creation, understanding the value equation is crucial. The value equation can be represented as follows: capital plus input plus business activities equals outputs and outcomes. This formula emphasises the relationship between capital (such as cash), inputs (such as raw materials or human resources), business activities (processes and operational data), and the resulting outputs and outcomes, which represent the company's performance and the products or services it produces.

Elements of Value Creation
The value creation process encompasses various elements, including financial, manufacturing, intellectual, human resources, social and relationship, and natural resources. These elements contribute to the inputs required for the value creation process. By considering the activities, outputs, and outcomes associated with these elements, organisations can better understand how value is created within their operations.

Value Creation Example
A simple example to illustrate value creation is the process of transforming oranges into orange juice. Suppose we purchase inexpensive oranges for one pound. To add value, we squeeze the oranges to extract the juice and package it in cartons. These activities represent the process, with the input being the oranges and the output being the juice. By transforming the raw material into a finished product, we can sell a carton of orange juice for three pounds, thereby creating value through the production process.

Value creation is about adding value to processes within an organisation. By understanding the value equation and considering the elements involved in value creation, organisations can optimise their operations and enhance their performance. The example of transforming oranges into orange juice illustrates how value can be created by leveraging inputs, business activities, and producing desirable outputs.

Chapter 11 - Internal Controls & Audit

Introduction to Internal Audit

An internal audit is an essential component of an organisation's governance and risk management processes. It serves as an independent appraisal activity that is established within the organisation. In this chapter, we will explore the definition, main roles, and functions of an internal audit.

An internal audit can be defined as an independent appraisal activity that objectively evaluates an organisation's operations, financial systems, and internal controls. By conducting regular audits, the internal audit department provides assurance to management and stakeholders that the organisation's resources are utilised effectively and efficiently.

Roles and Functions of Internal Audit

The internal audit department performs several vital roles and functions within an organisation. These include:

Review of Accounting and Internal Control Systems: The internal audit department conducts thorough assessments of the organisation's accounting practices and internal control systems. By reviewing these systems, they ensure that the organisation's financial information is accurate, reliable, and compliant with applicable standards.

Examination of Financial and Operating Information: Internal auditors analyse financial statements, budgets, and other operational information to identify any irregularities or areas of concern. This examination helps management make informed decisions and take appropriate corrective actions.

Risk Identification: Internal auditors assist in identifying and evaluating risks faced by the organisation. By conducting risk assessments, they contribute to the development of effective risk management strategies and provide recommendations to mitigate potential risks.

Special Investigations: In cases where fraud or other irregular activities are suspected, the internal audit department conducts special investigations. These investigations aim to uncover any fraudulent practices, assess their impact on the organisation, and recommend measures to prevent similar incidents in the future.

Compliance Review: Internal auditors review the organisation's compliance with laws, regulations, and internal policies. By ensuring compliance, they help protect the organisation from legal and reputational risks.

Evaluation of Operations: The internal audit department evaluates the economy, efficiency, and effectiveness of the organisation's operations. Through this evaluation, they identify opportunities for improvement, cost savings, and optimisation of resources.

Organisations Requiring Internal Audit

Determining whether an organisation requires an internal audit department depends on several characteristics. While the assessment can be subjective, the following factors indicate the need for an internal audit:

Size and Complexity: Larger and more complex organisations often require an internal audit department to ensure comprehensive oversight of their operations, financial systems, and internal controls.

Number of Employees: Organisations with a significant number of employees may benefit from an internal audit department to address the challenges associated with managing and monitoring a large workforce.

High-Risk Events: Organisations experiencing frequent high-risk events, such as accidents resulting in injuries or environmental spills, would benefit from an internal audit department to assess the causes, impacts, and preventive measures related to such incidents.

Internal Control Problems: Organisations with severe internal control deficiencies or a history of control failures should establish an internal audit department to address and rectify these issues.

Information Systems Changes: If an organisation undergoes significant changes in its information systems, an internal audit department can help ensure the successful implementation, integration, and security of these systems.

Financial Considerations: Conducting a cost-benefit analysis is crucial in determining the need for an internal audit department. Organisations with substantial financial resources and a high potential for financial risks should consider establishing an internal audit function.

Significance of Changes: Organisations undergoing significant changes, such as mergers, acquisitions, or restructuring, should evaluate the need for an internal audit department to address the associated risks and ensure a smooth transition.

An internal audit plays a critical role in providing independent assurance and advisory services to organisations. By examining financial information, evaluating internal controls, and identifying risks, an internal audit department enhances the overall governance and compliance framework of an organisation. The need for an internal audit department varies based on the organisation's size, complexity, risk profile, and financial considerations.

Maintaining independence is crucial for internal auditors to carry out their work objectively. In this chapter, we will explore the factors that protect an internal auditor's independence and identify potential ethical threats they may encounter.

To safeguard an internal auditor's independence, four main factors come into play:

1. **Independence from Executive Management**: It is essential for internal auditors to remain independent from executive management. This ensures that their evaluations and opinions are unbiased and not influenced by management's interests. The chief internal auditor should have direct access to the chairman, and the appointment and termination of the chief internal auditor should be approved by the audit committee, not the CEO.

2. **Audit Committee Oversight**: The audit committee plays a vital role in protecting auditor independence. By overseeing the internal audit function, the audit committee ensures that the internal auditors have the necessary authority, resources, and autonomy to perform their duties independently.

3. **Objectivity and Professional Scepticism**: Internal auditors must maintain a high level of objectivity and professional scepticism throughout their work. This means they approach their assessments with an impartial mindset, critically evaluating evidence, and not being unduly influenced by personal biases or external pressures.

4. **Code of Ethics and Professional Standards**: Internal auditors are guided by a code of ethics and professional standards, such as those issued by the Institute of Internal Auditors (IIA). Adhering to these standards reinforces their commitment to

objectivity, integrity, and independence in their work.

Ethical Threats to Auditor Independence

Various ethical threats can compromise an auditor's independence, whether real or perceived. Internal auditors should be aware of and address these threats to maintain their credibility and effectiveness. The main threats to auditor independence include:

Self-Interest: This threat arises when auditors act to benefit themselves financially or when their actions are influenced by the financial interests of the client. It is essential for auditors to prioritise objectivity and independence over personal or financial gain.

Familiarity: Long-term relationships or excessive familiarity with clients can compromise an auditor's independence. Maintaining professional distance and objectivity is crucial, even in long-standing client relationships.

Advocacy: Advocacy threats occur when auditors promote a specific opinion or position without genuinely believing it to be accurate or appropriate. Auditors must ensure that their opinions and recommendations are based on their professional judgment and the evidence at hand, rather than being swayed by external pressures.

Self-Review: Internal auditors should avoid reviewing their own work without appropriate oversight. Conducting self-reviews can undermine the objectivity and thoroughness of the audit process. Independent review and validation are essential to maintain the integrity of the audit findings.

Intimidation: Intimidation threats arise when auditors face coercion, pressure, or threats from management or other stakeholders to alter their findings or opinions. It is crucial for auditors to resist such intimidation and report any attempts to compromise their independence.

By understanding and proactively addressing these ethical threats, internal auditors can uphold their independence, ensuring the credibility and integrity of their audit opinions and recommendations.

The Audit Committee and Internal Controls

Next, we will explore the crucial role of the audit committee in overseeing internal controls and how it aligns with the objectives of the board of directors, internal auditors, and external auditors.

The audit committee plays a vital role in ensuring effective corporate governance and oversight. Their main responsibilities can be summarised as review, oversee, monitor, and review again. Let's break it down further:

1. **Review**: The audit committee reviews the company's internal control systems and also evaluates the work of the external auditors to ensure compliance and accuracy.
2. **Oversee**: They oversee the work of the internal audit function, ensuring its independence and effectiveness. Additionally, they monitor the integrity of the financial statements and the company's internal control risk management systems.
3. **Monitor**: The audit committee is responsible for monitoring the effectiveness of the internal controls and assessing their efficiency. They receive reports from internal auditors on matters such as internal controls testing.

4. **Approve**: They review and approve statements in the annual report related to internal controls, risk management, and financial statements. They also review the company's strategy and risk appetite and discuss the effectiveness of internal controls with management.

Alignment of Audit Committee and Internal Controls

Whilst the objectives of the board of directors and audit committee regarding internal controls may not be the same, they should align.

The **board's** objectives include:

- Reviewing the company's strategy and risk appetite.
- Implementing internal audit recommendations.
- Discussing the effectiveness of internal controls with management.
- Reviewing and assessing the effectiveness of internal controls.

The **audit committee's** objectives, on the other hand, encompass:

- Reviewing the company's internal financial controls.
- Reviewing management's internal control risk management systems.
- Approving statements related to internal controls in the annual report.
- Receiving reports from internal audit on internal controls testing.

Alignment of Audit Committee with Internal and External Auditors

The audit committee also plays a crucial role in overseeing the work of both internal and external auditors.

With internal auditors:

- They oversee the work of the internal audit function, ensuring its effectiveness.
- They monitor and assess the internal audit's annual work plan.
- They approve the appointment of the head of internal audit to preserve independence.
- They check the efficiency of internal audit activities and ensure recommendations are acted upon.
- They ensure accountability of the internal audit function to the audit committee.

Regarding external auditors:

- The audit committee is responsible for the appointment of external auditors.
- They oversee the selection process for new external auditors.
- They approve the terms of communication, engagement, and remuneration of external auditors.
- They ensure the independence and objectivity of the external auditors.
- They review the scope and plans for the audit, from its beginning to completion.

Importance of Internal Controls & Audit Committees to Shareholders

Strong internal controls are essential for shareholder confidence and trust in a company's financial statements. Shareholders expect companies to have sound internal control systems in place to safeguard their investments. Without robust internal controls, the credibility of the annual report and financial statements is at risk.

What is the significance of an Audit Committee to shareholders?

1. The Chair of the Audit Committee must be available at the annual general meeting (AGM) to address shareholder questions.
2. Shareholders have the right to know whether sufficient internal controls are in place to protect their investments.
3. The annual report explains the work of the Audit Committee, covering all material controls and risk management systems.
4. The Board should conduct an annual review of internal control systems to provide shareholders with necessary information and assurance.

The Sarbanes-Oxley Act and Internal Controls

Next, we will discuss the significance of the Sarbanes-Oxley Act and discuss internal controls. We will explore the purposes, roles, and responsibilities associated with maintaining sound internal control systems.

The Sarbanes-Oxley Act (SOX) is a legislation that imposes detailed legal reporting requirements. This section will provide a comprehensive understanding of the key elements in The SOX Act, specifically; internal controls, sound internal control systems, and the roles and responsibilities involved in monitoring and identifying risks and controls within an internal control environment.

Internal Control Roles and Responsibilities

The Board of Directors holds the responsibility for maintaining a robust system of internal controls. The purpose of this system is to safeguard the primary stakeholders, which, in this case, are the shareholders. The directors should implement policies to ensure the establishment of a sound internal control system. Ideally, this system should be reviewed on an annual basis.

Controls serve as mechanisms to minimise risks within an organisation. They are designed to ensure that risks are mitigated and managed effectively.

Internal Control Systems and Internal Management Controls

An internal control system refers to a network of systems established within a company or organisation to provide reasonable assurance that organisational objectives can be achieved. On the other hand, internal management controls encompass the procedures and policies in place to ensure the accomplishment of a company's objectives.

Multiple stakeholders are involved in risk management and internal control, beyond just the directors. The CEO bears ultimate responsibility for internal control systems, supported by the board of directors, a risk committee, executive management, heads of business units, and internal auditors. Internal auditors evaluate the effectiveness of controls and provide recommendations for improvement. External auditors advise on the establishment and monitoring of internal controls. However, it is the responsibility of all employees within a company or organisation to operate and adhere to internal control procedures.

Objectives and Benefits of Internal Control Systems

The objectives of internal control systems and reporting are to ensure the orderly and efficient conduct of business, safeguard assets, prevent and detect fraud or errors, ensure accuracy and completeness of accounting records, and ensure timely preparation of financial information.

The benefits of internal control systems include ensuring the effectiveness and efficiency of operations, reliability of financial reporting, and compliance with laws and regulations to avoid fines.

Characteristics of an Appropriate Control System

When we refer to a sound control system, we mean an appropriate control system. Let's explore the key characteristics of a good control system.

Embedded within Operations
A strong control system is not treated as a separate exercise or a mere tick-box exercise. Instead, it is embedded within the operations of the business. This means that controls are integrated into the daily operations and processes, becoming an integral part of how the organisation functions.

Responsive to Changing Risks
Organisations with sound control systems are able to respond effectively to changing risks, both within and outside the company. This requires a proactive approach to identify and assess risks, and to adapt control measures accordingly. It ensures that controls remain relevant and effective in mitigating emerging risks.

Reporting of Failures and Weaknesses

Sound control systems include procedures for reporting any failures or weaknesses in controls. This fosters a culture of transparency and accountability, where issues can be identified, addressed, and learned from. It allows for timely corrective actions to be taken to strengthen the control environment.

Elements of Effective Internal Control Systems

Effective internal control systems encompass five key classifications or elements. Familiarising ourselves with these elements is essential for understanding internal control systems.

Control Environment

The tone tends to be set at the top by senior leadership and consequentially plays a crucial role in the control environment. A sound control environment is established when management demonstrates a commitment to controls and fosters a culture where all employees, from top to bottom, recognise the importance of controls.

Risk Assessment

Risk assessment involves setting objectives for the organisation and considering both internal and external risks. It requires distinguishing between controllable and uncontrollable risks and implementing appropriate measures to manage and mitigate those risks.

Control Activities

Control activities involve the policies and procedures in place to ensure that decisions and instructions from management can be carried out effectively at all levels of the organisation. These controls provide a framework for operational activities and help maintain compliance with established policies.

Information and Communication

Information and communication are vital components of a robust control system. It involves ensuring that correct and relevant information is communicated to the right individuals within the organisation. Quality information systems are essential for providing internal and external information necessary for effective decision-making.

Monitoring

Monitoring is an ongoing process that ensures control systems are appropriate and reliable. Internal audit plays a significant role in carrying out monitoring activities, assessing the effectiveness of controls, and identifying areas for improvement.

A sound control system is one that is embedded within operations, responsive to changing risks, and includes reporting procedures for failures and weaknesses. The key elements of an effective internal control system are the control environment, risk assessment, control activities, information and communication, and monitoring. Understanding and implementing these elements are vital for establishing strong internal controls within an organisation.

Information Flows for Management

In the context of control systems, understanding how information flows within an organisation is crucial. Let's explore the three management levels and their respective responsibilities for internal controls, risks, and information systems.

Operational Level

At the operational level, internal controls and risks must be identified and addressed. This level focuses on the day-to-day activities of the organisation. Operational managers need access to information that enables them to report on weaknesses in controls and recommend risk-mitigating measures.

Tactical Level
The tactical level is responsible for managing risks from a broader perspective. Managers at this level must be able to assess risks, establish internal controls, and make informed decisions based on the available information. They play a vital role in implementing risk management strategies.

Strategic Level
The highest level of management, the strategic level, focuses on assessing risks and reviewing the effectiveness of internal controls. Strategic managers analyse the overall risk landscape of the organisation and ensure that appropriate controls are in place to mitigate those risks.

Fraud and Risk Management Strategy

Developing a robust risk management strategy for fraud is essential. There are three key elements that should be included in such a strategy: fraud prevention, fraud detection, and fraud response.

Fraud Prevention
To prevent fraud, organisations should foster an anti-fraud culture, provide risk awareness training, establish whistleblowing mechanisms, and implement sound internal control systems. These measures help create a deterrent environment and minimise the opportunity for fraudulent activities.

Fraud Detection
Detecting fraud requires regular checks and monitoring. Examples include performing routine stocktaking, reconciling cash accounts, and implementing other detection

mechanisms. Timely detection can help mitigate losses and prevent further damage.

Fraud Response

When fraud is suspected or detected, organisations need to have a well-defined response plan. This involves dealing with suspected cases through established procedures, gathering evidence, and providing support for decision-making and potential legal actions. Responses may include criminal prosecution, civil litigation, and internal disciplinary actions.

The organisation's response to fraud should be comprehensive, aiming to address the issue and hold responsible parties accountable.

Information flows within an organisation at different management levels, supporting internal controls and risk management. Developing a risk management strategy for fraud involves prevention, detection, and response. By implementing preventive measures, detecting fraudulent activities, and having a robust response plan, organisations can effectively manage the risks associated with fraud.

Chapter 12 – Risks & Risk Management

A risk can be defined as a potential future loss that may occur due to a current action or inaction. It involves unrealised future losses resulting from present decisions or lack thereof. In essence, risks encompass both opportunities and dangers associated with uncertain future events, emphasising a forward-looking approach.

Taking risks is often correlated with potential rewards. By accepting risks, individuals or organisations can gain a competitive advantage, increase financial returns, or reap other benefits.

Types of Risk Management

Risk management involves two primary categories: downside risks and upside risks.

Downside risks involve identifying new risks and assessing changes in existing risks. The focus is on minimising negative consequences and preventing potential losses.

Upside risks, on the other hand, involve recognising and maximising opportunities. This entails making the best use of favourable circumstances to enhance outcomes.

Risk management is a systematic process aimed at reducing adverse consequences by decreasing the likelihood of their occurrence. Throughout this chapter, the two key variables we will emphasise are likelihood and impact – both are essential factors in risk management.

Responsibility for Risk Management

Generally, the responsibility for risk management lies with management or the organisation itself. Risk management systems involve various steps:

- **Risk Identification:** This entails compiling a comprehensive list of potential risks within the organisation.
- **Risk Assessment**: Prioritising the identified risks based on their severity and potential impact.
- **Risk Planning:** Developing strategies to avoid risks and creating contingency plans or backup options.
- **Risk Monitoring:** Conducting regular risk audits to assess how risks are managed, determining which risks are effectively addressed, and identifying any unmanaged risks.

Enterprise Risk Management (ERM)

In larger organisations, an ERM framework may be established. ERM stands for Enterprise Risk Management, and it aligns risk management practices with the organisation's business strategy. ERM emphasises that risk management is the responsibility of everyone within the organisation, much like controls. It fosters a risk-aware culture and considers a broad range of risks from strategic, financial, operational, and compliance perspectives.

The Role of the Board and Risk Culture

Within an ERM approach, the board plays a crucial role in leading the focused risk management strategy. Risk management should be integrated into the organisation's culture, emphasising the importance of embedding risk awareness throughout the organisation.

Differentiating Strategic and Operational Risks

When identifying risks from a strategic and operational standpoint, there are notable differences:

Strategic risks arise from strategic decisions and their consequences. These risks result from the positioning of a company within its environment, such as failing to enhance existing systems, products, or services. They are primarily assessed and managed at the senior management level.

Operational risks stem from business operations and internal controls. They include losses resulting from inadequate or failed internal controls, fraud, quality control failures, and production issues. Operational risks are identified at an operational level and managed through internal control systems.

Understanding Business Risks

Business risks are strategic in nature and pose a threat to the overall health and survival of the entire business. These risks encompass factors that can jeopardise the well-being and continuity of the business.

Types of Business Risks

Several types of business risks exist, including market risks, credit risks, health and safety risks, financial risks (such as running out of funds), legal risks, technological risks, reputational risks, and more. It is crucial to be aware of these various types and be able to identify them when analysing a case study.

Relative Risk Factors and Related Risks

Relative risk factors are risks that are connected in some way. Related risks can vary due to the presence of another risk or when two risks share a common cause. Risk correlation is significant in understanding the relationship between risks. Positive correlation means that as one risk increases, another risk also increases. On the other hand, negative correlation implies that as one risk increases, another risk decreases.

Risk Assessments

There are several methods for conducting risk assessments, such as using a risk map or a risk heat map. A risk map illustrates the impact on the organisation and the likelihood of a risk occurring, enabling the prioritisation of risks. Risks with high impact and high likelihood require urgent attention. Impact refers to the severity or hazardous nature of a risk, while likelihood represents the probability of its occurrence. A risk heat map combines the risk level with the likelihood of a risk, helping identify risks that demand immediate attention based on their extreme impact and high probability.

Managing, Monitoring, and Mitigating Risks

The primary responsibility of the board of directors in risk management is to consider risks at a strategic level and establish the organisation's risk appetite and approach. Additionally, the board plays other roles, such as setting risk attitudes and capacities, monitoring risk management plans, and determining residual risk. Mitigating risk involves implementing strategies and measures to minimise the adverse impact of risks and prevent potential losses.

Risk management is an ongoing process that requires continuous monitoring and evaluation. It involves identifying, analysing, assessing, and responding to risks to ensure the organisation can effectively navigate uncertainties and protect its interests.

Framework for Board Consideration of Risk

Business Strategy and Risk Appetite

The board's approach to risk management follows a specific framework, which involves several steps. It begins with defining the business strategy, which outlines the actions and direction the company will pursue. The business strategy then leads to determining the risk appetite, which refers to the level of risk the company is willing to accept. This includes establishing the risk strategy, which outlines how risks will be managed. Finally, the framework considers residual risks— risks that cannot be effectively managed.

Role of the Risk Manager

The risk manager holds a crucial position within the Risk Management Committee and reports directly to the board of directors. Their primary responsibility is to implement risk management policies. Other tasks include identifying and evaluating risks, implementing and monitoring risk mitigation strategies, improving risk management processes, assisting external and internal auditors, collaborating with risk committees and the board, and developing and implementing risk management programs.

Role of the Risk Committee

The main objectives of the Risk Committee are to raise risk awareness and ensure that processes are in place for identifying, reporting, and monitoring risks. They are also responsible for updating the company's risk profile. In summary, the key tasks of the Risk Committee involve increasing risk awareness, establishing risk management policies, implementing monitoring and reporting processes, and updating the company's risk profile and risk appetite.

Embedding Risk into the Organisation

Embedding risk within the organisation is crucial to ensure that it becomes an integral part of the way business is conducted. It should be considered at two levels: as part of the overall control system and as part of any applicable legislative or regulatory framework. The process of embedding risk involves identifying existing controls within the organisation, monitoring and improving risks, and documenting the controls and risks once they have been tested. Performance metrics are typically used to effectively monitor risks.

Embedding Risk into Organisational Culture

To establish a strong risk culture within the organisation, it is important to create risk awareness among employees and enable them to recognise risks when they occur. All employees should be encouraged to follow risk management policies, making them all risk managers in their respective roles. This responsibility should be driven from top-tier management, fostering an open culture for discussing and managing risks. Additionally, utilising metrics for early risk warning, including risk management responsibilities in job descriptions, informing staff about the need for risk management, and sharing success stories are effective strategies for embedding risk into the organisational culture.

Risk Mapping

Risk mapping is a process that involves assessing and visualising risks based on their impact and likelihood. It provides a comprehensive overview of the organisation's risk landscape, allowing for effective risk management and decision-making. By mapping risks, businesses can prioritise their focus and allocate resources accordingly.

Impact and Likelihood
When considering risk mapping, two key factors come into play: impact and likelihood.

Impact refers to the potential consequences or severity of a risk event. It assesses the extent to which the risk could harm the organisation, its objectives, or its stakeholders. High-impact risks have the potential to cause significant damage, while low-impact risks may have a lesser effect.

Likelihood evaluates the probability or chance of a risk event occurring. It considers the frequency or occurrence rate of the risk. Risks with a high likelihood are more likely to happen, while risks with a low likelihood are less probable.

Risk Matrix

Risk mapping often involves the use of a risk matrix, which is a visual representation of risks based on their impact and likelihood. The risk matrix typically consists of a grid with different levels of impact and likelihood, dividing risks into categories such as high, medium, and low.

For example, a risk matrix may have five levels of impact (ranging from catastrophic to insignificant) and five levels of likelihood (ranging from frequent to rare). By plotting each risk on the matrix, it becomes easier to prioritise risks and determine appropriate risk responses.

Risk Response Strategies

Once risks have been mapped and categorised, organisations can apply suitable risk response strategies. Here are examples of response strategies based on different risk categories:

- **High Impact, High Likelihood (Avoid):** Risks falling into this category pose significant threats and are likely to occur. The recommended strategy is to avoid these risks whenever possible. For instance, if a product poses a high risk to consumer safety, the organisation may choose to discontinue its production or invest heavily in improvements to eliminate the risk.
- **Low Impact, High Likelihood (Reduce):** These risks may have a lower potential impact but are still likely to occur frequently. The focus here is on reducing the likelihood or consequences of the risk. For instance, implementing regular equipment maintenance procedures can help reduce the likelihood of machinery breakdowns.
- **High Impact, Low Likelihood (Transfer):** Risks with high impact but low likelihood can be transferred to external parties, such as insurance companies or subcontractors. By transferring the risk, the organisation minimises its financial exposure. For example, an organisation might purchase insurance coverage for potential natural disasters to mitigate the financial impact of such events.
- **Low Impact, Low Likelihood (Accept):** Risks falling into this category have minimal potential impact and are unlikely to occur frequently. Organisations may choose to accept these risks without significant intervention. For example, if a risk poses a negligible impact on the organisation's operations and has a low probability of occurring, it may be deemed acceptable without requiring additional resources for mitigation.

By applying these risk response strategies based on the risk mapping exercise, organisations can effectively manage their risks and align their resources accordingly. Risk mapping facilitates a proactive and systematic approach to risk management, enabling businesses to make informed decisions to protect their interests.

The acronym TARA (Transfer, Avoid, Reduce, Accept) can be used to remember these risk mitigation strategies.

Diversifying Risk

Diversifying risk is another strategy to consider, aiming to reduce overall risk exposure. This involves spreading risk across different areas or stakeholders.

- **Horizontal Integration**: Passing the risk onto competitors or similar businesses.
- **Backward Integration**: Transferring risk to suppliers or upstream partners.
- **Forward Integration**: Sharing risk with distribution outlets or downstream partners.

Diversification can be either related or unrelated:

- **Related Diversification**: Expanding beyond the current product and market within the same industry.
- **Unrelated Diversification**: Expanding into products and markets that may not have a direct relationship to the current offerings.

Risk Monitoring and Auditing

Risk monitoring, also known as risk auditing, provides an independent evaluation of risks and controls within an organisation. This process involves:

1. **Identifying risks:** Identifying potential risks that may impact the organisation's objectives.

2. **Assessing risks**: Evaluating the likelihood and potential impact of identified risks.
3. **Reviewing controls**: Examining the effectiveness of existing controls in mitigating risks.
4. **Reporting findings**: Reporting on inadequate risks and suggesting improvements to enhance risk management processes.

Risk monitoring and auditing can be conducted internally or externally by independent audit teams, ensuring an unbiased assessment of risks and controls.

Assurance Mapping in Risk Management

Assurance mapping is a methodology used in risk management to systematically identify and map the sources and types of assurances across the four lines of defence. It provides a structured approach to ensure that the organisation has appropriate measures in place to manage risks effectively.

The Four Lines of Defence

The concept of the four lines of defence is a widely recognised framework in risk management. It delineates the various roles and responsibilities within an organisation for managing and mitigating risks.

1. **First Line of Defence**: This refers to the operational level where risks are managed on a day-to-day basis by employees directly involved in business processes. It includes individuals responsible for executing risk management activities and maintaining controls within their respective areas of responsibility. The first line of defence plays a crucial role in identifying, assessing, and mitigating risks at the operational level.

2. **Second Line of Defence**: The second line of defence involves oversight functions that ensure the effectiveness of risk management across the organisation. This includes risk management departments, compliance functions, and other control functions. They establish policies, procedures, and frameworks to guide risk management practices, monitor compliance, and provide guidance and support to the first line of defence. The second line of defence helps to ensure that risks are managed in a consistent and controlled manner.

3. **Third Line of Defence**: The third line of defence comprises objective and independent assurance providers. Internal audit functions are a key component of the third line of defence. They assess the effectiveness of risk management practices, evaluate internal controls, and provide independent assurance to the organisation's management and board of directors. Internal auditors offer an unbiased evaluation of risk management processes and help identify areas for improvement.

4. **Fourth Line of Defence**: The fourth line of defence includes external auditors who provide independent assurance to stakeholders outside the organisation. They assess the organisation's financial statements, controls, and overall risk management practices. External auditors provide an external perspective on the organisation's risk management and help ensure transparency and accountability.

Assurance Mapping Process

Assurance mapping involves systematically identifying and mapping the sources of assurance across the four lines of defence. This process helps ensure that there is adequate coverage and coordination of assurance activities throughout the organisation.

The methodology includes:

1. **Identification of Assurances**: Identifying the various sources and types of assurances within each line of defence. This includes documentation, policies, procedures, controls, and other mechanisms that provide assurance regarding risk management practices.
2. **Mapping of Assurances**: Mapping the identified assurances to the respective lines of defence. This helps visualise the distribution and coverage of assurances within the organisation and ensures that there are no gaps or overlaps in assurance provision.
3. **Evaluation of Assurance Effectiveness**: Assessing the effectiveness and reliability of the identified assurances. This involves evaluating the design and implementation of assurance mechanisms to determine their adequacy in managing and mitigating risks effectively.
4. **Improvement and Enhancement**: Identifying opportunities for improvement and enhancement of assurance mechanisms. This may involve strengthening controls, revising policies and procedures, or implementing additional assurance activities where necessary.

By conducting assurance mapping, organisations can gain a comprehensive understanding of their assurance framework, ensure proper coordination and coverage of assurances, and enhance their overall risk management capabilities.

Chapter 13 – Ethics & Professionalism

In this chapter, we will explore the concepts of ethics, professionalism, and the importance of acting in the public interest. Understanding these principles is vital for individuals in professions such as accounting to maintain their integrity and fulfil their responsibilities to society.

Definitions

Profession

A profession is characterised by a body of theory and knowledge that is utilised to support the public interest. It involves a collective understanding of practices, standards, and expertise that contribute to the well-being of society as a whole.

Professionalism

Professionalism refers to the manner in which individuals act to support the public interest. Acting professionally involves upholding ethical codes of conduct and demonstrating a sense of duty and responsibility towards society.

Public Interest

Acting in the public interest means making decisions and taking actions that benefit society, rather than serving individual interests. It entails considering the greater good and the impact of decisions on society's well-being.

Business Ethics and Stakeholders

Having power and influence involves playing a crucial role in upholding ethical standards and acting in the public interest.

They are guided by ethical codes that prohibit actions against the public interest. However, determining whether to disclose certain information requires careful evaluation of each situation's merits, as there is no one-size-fits-all rule.

Responsible Leadership
Responsible leadership encompasses making informed ethical decisions, displaying moral courage, and striving for positive change. It involves forward-looking thinking, effective communication with stakeholders, and engaging in collective problem-solving rather than pursuing individual interests.

Business ethics have a significant impact on various stakeholders:

- **Shareholders**: Expect fair and proper returns on their investments and transparency regarding the management of shareholder investments.
- **Suppliers**: Desire timely delivery of quality goods.
- **Customers**: Seek fair treatment, recognition, and the provision of high-quality products and services.
- **Employees**: Value fair treatment, adequate compensation, a safe and healthy work environment, and opportunities for training and development.
- **Wider Community**: Corporate social responsibility practices influence society at large, and CSR reports outline how organisations engage with the community.

Professional Code of Ethics
The professional code of ethics serves as a guide for ethical behaviour in a specific profession. It typically consists of four fundamental components:

1. **Introduction**: Describes who the code applies to and how it is enforced.

2. **Fundamental Principles**: Outlines key principles that all members of the profession must adhere to.
3. **Conceptual Framework**: Explains how the principles should be applied in practice.
4. **Detailed Application**: Provides guidance on applying the principles to specific situations.

Fundamental Ethical Principles

The Professional Code of Conduct encompasses five fundamental ethical principles:

1. **Integrity**: Emphasises being honest and straightforward in professional dealings.
2. **Objectivity**: Requires avoiding bias or conflicts of interest and maintaining impartiality in decision-making.
3. **Competence**: Involves the duty to continuously update and maintain professional knowledge and skills at an appropriate level.
4. **Confidentiality**: Demands not disclosing information without prior consent or legal obligation.
5. **Professional Behaviour**: Requires compliance with relevant laws, regulations, and standards, as well as avoiding actions that bring disrepute to the profession.

Benefits and Drawbacks of a Code of Ethics

A corporate code of ethics or a professional code of ethics offers several benefits, including providing a framework for conflict resolution, offering guidelines for ethical disputes, and establishing boundaries that should not be crossed. However, there are also drawbacks, such as subjectivity in interpretation, the potential mismatch between the code and specific ethical issues, and the lack of clear or effective punishment for code breaches.

Ethical Threats and Safeguards

To maintain ethical standards, it is important to identify and address potential ethical threats. Safeguards can be implemented to mitigate these threats, ensuring that professionals can uphold their ethical obligations effectively.

A threat refers to a situation in which an individual is tempted to deviate from the established Code of Ethics. It arises when there is a potential conflict between personal interests or external pressures and the ethical standards and principles that guide professional conduct.

The Main Safeguards

There are three primary types of safeguards that can help mitigate or eliminate threats to ethical behaviour:

1. **Professional safeguards**: These safeguards pertain to the individual's profession and the requirements set forth by relevant regulatory bodies. Continuous Professional Development (CPD) is an important aspect of professional safeguarding, which involves ongoing education, training, and skill development. Additionally, disciplinary proceedings play a crucial role in upholding ethical standards within the profession.
2. **Work environment safeguards**: These safeguards focus on creating an ethical work environment within an organisation. They include the establishment and implementation of internal control systems to monitor and assess ethical conduct, review procedures to evaluate compliance with ethical standards, and the existence of a well-defined Code of Ethics that outlines expected behaviours. Disciplinary procedures ensure that violations of ethical standards are appropriately addressed.

3. **Individual safeguards**: Individuals can take personal responsibility for maintaining ethical conduct. They can seek guidance and mentoring from more experienced professionals, comply with relevant professional standards and regulations, and actively engage with their professional body, for support and guidance.

Exploring Bribery and Corruption

Corruption involves bribery and any other actions taken by individuals entrusted with responsibilities in either the public or private domain, which violate their duties and aim to secure undue advantages for themselves or others. Bribery refers to the act of offering, promising, giving, requesting, agreeing to receive, accepting, or bribing a foreign public official.

In the context of corruption, certain keywords and concepts are important to consider. Corruption can be seen as a form of bribery, where individuals seek personal benefits by disregarding their obligations and responsibilities. Examples of corrupt practices include providing excessive hospitality, such as offering high-value gifts, entertainment, or perks to influence business decisions. Another example is when a mining company pays a substantial amount of money to government officials to obtain mining rights, which can be seen as an unethical and corrupt act.

Understanding the UK Bribery Act

The UK Bribery Act, passed in 2010, addresses the issue of bribery and sets out four offences under its purview:

1. **Offering, promising, or giving a** bribe: This offence encompasses the act of providing or attempting to provide a bribe to another person.

2. **Requesting, agreeing to receive, or accepting a bribe**: This offence relates to the act of soliciting or accepting a bribe from another person.
3. **Bribing a foreign public official**: This offence specifically involves offering, promising, or giving a bribe to a foreign public official to influence their actions or decisions.
4. **Failing to prevent bribery**: This corporate offence holds organisations liable if they fail to prevent bribery by associated persons, such as employees or agents.

Even the failure to prevent bribery can lead to legal consequences in the UK.

Dealing With Ethical Conflicts

When confronted with ethical conflicts, it is essential to approach them in a systematic manner and consider several factors:

- **Gathering relevant information**: This involves collecting as much information as possible about the ethical conflict, including identifying the ethical issues involved, establishing the facts of the situation, examining the fundamental principles that apply, and considering the available alternative courses of action. It is also important to review the established internal procedures within the organisation.
- **Deciding on a course of action**: After gathering information, individuals should carefully consider their options. This may involve deciding to withdraw from the engagement or assignment that poses the ethical conflict. Seeking advice from professional institutions, such as the Chartered Accountants or Legal Professionals can provide valuable guidance. Consulting with appropriate individuals within the

organisation, including colleagues and those charged with governance, can also help in making an informed decision. Lastly, it is crucial to evaluate the potential consequences of each possible course of action.

Factors Influencing Ethical Decision-Making

The ability to make ethical decisions is influenced by two categories of factors: issue-related factors and context-related factors.

1. **Issue-related factors**: These factors relate to the specific ethical issue at hand and its impact on the decision-maker. Factors affecting moral intensity include the moral framing of the situation, proximity to those affected by the decision, temporal immediacy (how soon the effects of the decision occur), concentration of effect (how many people are impacted), magnitude of consequences, agreement with ethical norms, and the probability of harm or benefit resulting from the decision.

2. **Context-related factors**: These factors pertain to the broader context in which ethical decisions are made. They include the system of rewards within the organisation, as rewards based solely on achievement may incentivise unethical behaviour. The influence of authority figures, such as senior managers, can also impact the ethical climate within an organisation. Bureaucracy and adherence to rules and procedures can either support or hinder ethical decision-making. Work roles and group norms can influence an individual's perception of what is considered ethical. Finally, cultural factors can vary across different societies, and cultural norms may shape ethical decision-making processes.

By considering both issue-related and context-related factors, individuals can better navigate ethical conflicts and make informed decisions aligned with ethical principles.

Chapter 14 - Organisational Structure

This chapter focuses on organising for success and organisational structures. Let's explore how organisation contributes to success and discuss the various types of organisational structures, along with their advantages and disadvantages.

The Link Between Structure and Strategy

The connection between structure and strategy is significant. They are closely intertwined, and it is important to understand that structure can impact strategy, and vice versa. As strategies change, so does the structure. Elements such as specialisations, specialists, levels of authority, and bureaucracy often adapt to align with new strategies.

The Impact of Structure on Strategy

The degree of flexibility within an organisation, the level of specialist skills required, decision-making processes, innovation and knowledge management, as well as the development and support of critical success factors (CSF's), and market focus all influence the strategy. For instance, a more flexible organisational structure can foster fluid and efficient innovation, which aligns with the strategy. However, greater flexibility may also result in looser controls and an increased risk of fraud.

Understanding the Elements

To gain a better understanding of these elements, let's take a closer look at one example. An organisation with a flexible structure tends to facilitate smoother innovation processes, benefiting the strategy. On the other hand, it may lead to looser controls, potentially increasing the risk of fraudulent activities. It is crucial to consider how each element, including flexibility, specialist skills, innovation, critical factors, and market focus, can potentially impact the strategy. The key takeaway here is that strategy can influence structure and vice versa.

The Four Main Types of Organisational Structures

There are four primary types of organisational structures to consider.

1. The first is an **entrepreneurial structure**, which revolves around the owner or manager. This structure is commonly found in small businesses or start-ups where the owner is closely involved in all aspects of the company.

2. Moving on to slightly larger organisations, we have a **functional structure**. In this type of structure, groups of employees perform similar tasks, allowing for efficient coordination and specialisation.

3. A **divisional structure** is typically adopted by larger organisations. It involves splitting the company into several divisions based on product lines or geographic regions. This structure allows for greater focus and specialisation within each division.

4. Finally, the **matrix structure** is the largest type of organisational structure. It combines elements of both the divisional and functional structures. With this structure, the organisation is divided into divisions based on product lines or geographic regions, while groups of employees with similar skills and expertise work together. The matrix structure provides the advantages of both specialisation and coordination.

Mintzberg, a notable figure, developed a model known as the Mintzberg building blocks[6]. According to Mintzberg, as a business and its structure grow, different building blocks become increasingly important. He identified five types of building blocks: strategic apex, technostructure, operating core, middle line, and support staff.

1. **The Strategic Apex:** The strategic apex seeks direction and provides supervision. The structure in which it dominates is a simple structure.

2. **The Technostructure:** The technostructure aims for efficiency and provides procedures and standards. The structure in which it is most dominant is a machine bureaucracy.

3. **The Operating Core:** The operating core aims for proficiency and provides expertise and skills. The structure in which it dominates is a professional bureaucracy.

4. **The Middle Line:** The middle line desires concentration and provides focus and control. The structure in which it dominates is divisional.

5. **The Support Staff:** The support staff desires learning and provides help and training. They do not require a specific structure.

---

[6] Mintzberg, H. (1991). The effective organization: forces and forms. MIT Sloan Management Review, 32(2), 54.

Boundaryless Organisations

Boundaryless organisations are characterised by reduced hierarchy and functional separation. These organisations often foster innovation. There are three types of boundaryless organisations: the hollow structure, the modular structure, and the virtual structure. The hollow structure outsources noncore activities, the modular structure outsources specific parts of production, and the virtual structure involves collaboration between different organisational parts.

Business Process Outsourcing

Moving on to the topic of outsourcing, specifically business process outsourcing, let's explore its advantages and disadvantages. Outsourcing involves contracting a third-party company to handle certain functions, such as finance for a mug manufacturing company.

Advantages of Outsourcing

- **Cost Savings**: Outsourcing can often lead to significant cost savings. By outsourcing non-core functions, businesses can avoid investing in additional infrastructure, technology, and resources required to perform those tasks in-house. Outsourcing also allows access to economies of scale and lower labour costs in different regions or countries.
- **Focus on Core Activities**: Outsourcing enables businesses to focus their time, energy, and resources on their core competencies and strategic activities. By delegating non-core functions to specialised service providers, management can concentrate on key areas that directly contribute to their business objectives and competitive advantage.

- **Improved Efficiency and Expertise**: Outsourcing certain tasks to specialised providers can result in increased efficiency and access to expert knowledge and skills. Service providers often have extensive experience, streamlined processes, and industry-specific expertise, leading to improved quality, productivity, and innovation.
- **Scalability and Flexibility**: Outsourcing allows businesses to scale their operations up or down based on demand fluctuations. Service providers can quickly adjust resources and capacities to meet changing business needs, providing greater flexibility compared to maintaining in-house teams.
- **Risk Mitigation**: Sharing risks with outsourcing partners is another advantage. Service providers often assume responsibility for managing and mitigating risks associated with their specific areas of expertise, such as compliance, security, or technology upgrades. This can provide businesses with peace of mind and reduced exposure to certain risks.

Disadvantages of Outsourcing

- **Loss of Control**: Outsourcing means handing over certain functions or processes to external parties. This can result in a perceived loss of control over critical activities, decision-making, and quality assurance. Maintaining effective communication and establishing clear performance metrics are crucial to address this challenge.
- **Dependency on Third Parties**: Relying on external service providers introduces a level of dependency. Businesses may become vulnerable to disruptions or delays caused by the outsourcing partner's performance issues, financial instability, or changes in their business operations. Mitigating this risk

requires thorough evaluation and selection of reliable and reputable service providers.

- **Communication and Cultural Challenges**: Outsourcing often involves working with partners from different regions or countries, which can lead to communication barriers and cultural differences. Language barriers, time zone differences, and contrasting work styles may hinder effective collaboration and require additional effort to establish strong working relationships.

- **Security and Data Privacy Risks**: When outsourcing certain functions, businesses may need to share sensitive data and information with third-party providers. This introduces potential risks related to data security, confidentiality breaches, intellectual property protection, and compliance with data privacy regulations. Robust contracts, agreements, and security measures should be in place to mitigate these risks.

- **Potential Quality and Service Issues**: Despite selecting reputable service providers, there is always a risk of quality and service delivery issues. Differences in work standards, inadequate monitoring, or lack of alignment with business goals can impact the quality and timeliness of the outsourced services. Clear expectations, performance metrics, and regular communication are vital to manage and address any such challenges.

It is important for businesses to carefully assess the advantages and disadvantages of outsourcing, considering their specific needs, goals, and risk tolerance. Proper planning, due diligence, and ongoing management are essential to ensure successful outsourcing partnerships.

Harmon's Process Strategy Matrix[7] is a strategy model that focuses on two variables: the strategic importance and the complexity of a process.

Strategic Importance and Complexity

Harmon suggests that when considering whether to outsource a process, we should assess the strategic importance and complexity of that process.

- **High Strategic Importance, High Complexity: Improve the process** - According to Harmon, if a process is both strategically important and complex, the best approach is to invest efforts in improving the process internally.
- **Low Strategic Importance, High Complexity: Outsource the process** - When a process has low strategic importance but is complex, Harmon recommends outsourcing it. This allows the organisation to leverage external expertise and resources while focusing internal efforts on more critical activities.
- **Low Complexity, Low Strategic Importance: Minimise resource usage** - For processes with low complexity and low strategic importance, the aim is to use minimal resources. These processes should be streamlined to ensure efficiency without dedicating excessive time or resources.
- **High Strategic Importance, Low Complexity: Automate the process** - Harmon suggests that processes with high strategic importance but low complexity should be automated. Automation can

---

[7] *Harmon, P. (2003). Business process change: a manager's guide to improving, redesigning, and automating processes. Morgan Kaufmann.*

improve efficiency, reduce errors, and free up resources for other critical activities.

The Logic Behind Harmon's Model

Harmon's model is based on the belief that processes with high strategic importance significantly contribute to the success of a product or service. Conversely, processes with low strategic importance are necessary but add little value. By aligning the complexity and strategic importance of processes, organisations can make informed decisions about improvement, outsourcing, resource allocation, or automation.

Business Process Redesign

Now let's explore the concept of business process redesign, which involves rethinking and optimising existing processes.

Common Problems in Processes

Several common problems can hinder process efficiency:

- **Unnecessary activities**: Some activities within a process may be redundant or unnecessary, leading to inefficiencies and waste.
- **Incorrect order of activities**: In some cases, the sequence of activities may be incorrect, causing delays or suboptimal outcomes.
- Missing steps: Important steps or activities may be missing from the process, leading to gaps or errors.
- **Lengthy durations**: Processes that take too long can lead to bottlenecks, increased costs, and customer dissatisfaction.

Solutions to Process Problems

To address these problems, the following solutions can be applied:

- **Remove unnecessary activities**: Identify and eliminate activities that do not add value or contribute to the desired outcomes.
- Combine job roles and activities: Streamline processes by combining tasks and responsibilities where feasible, reducing duplication and improving efficiency.
- **Change the order of activities**: Assess the sequence of activities and reorganise them to optimise efficiency and improve outcomes.
- **Ensure no steps are missing**: Conduct a thorough review of the process to identify any missing steps or activities and incorporate them to ensure completeness.
- **Outsource activities**: For non-core or specialised activities, outsourcing can be considered as a solution, leveraging external expertise and resources.

It's essential to regularly review and redesign processes to ensure they remain efficient, effective, and aligned with business objectives.

Chapter 15 - Information Technology

This chapter focuses on the successful utilisation of information technology (IT) in various aspects of supply chain management (SCM). We will discuss upstream and downstream SCM, as well as the role of big data disruptive technologies, such as fintech, cloud technology, artificial intelligence, mobile technology, and corporate digital responsibility.

Supply Chain Management in IT

SCM, short for supply chain management, involves the reorganisation of various processes within an organisation. IT plays a crucial role in enabling greater information exchange between suppliers and customers, leading to improved efficiency and coordination. Here are a few benefits of SCM in IT:

- **Efficiency in Inventory Replenishment:** A practical example of smart IT integrated supply chain management is the automatic reordering process when a product is scanned at a supermarket checkout. As customers purchase items, the system sends notifications to suppliers, ensuring timely replenishment and inventory optimisation.

- **Coordination of New Product Development and Promotions:** SCM facilitated by IT allows better coordination of new product development and promotional activities. It enables dynamic pricing strategies, such as buy one, get one free, or automatic price reductions for slow-selling items, maximising customer engagement and profitability.

- **Greater Use of Outsourcing:** IT integration in SCM also leads to a greater use of outsourcing, allowing organisations to leverage external expertise and resources for non-core activities.

- **Facilitating the Shift from Push to Pull Systems:** IT enables the transition from push systems, where production decisions are led by manufacturers, to pull systems, where customer demands and preferences influence production. Pull systems aim for high personalisation and responsiveness to customer needs.

- **E-Procurement and Virtual Integration:** IT facilitates e-procurement, also known as online procurement, enabling better integration and interaction with customers. It fosters virtual integration, bringing customers and suppliers closer through online platforms.

Upstream and Downstream SCM

In supply chain management, the terms "upstream" and "downstream" are used to describe different stages or directions within the flow of materials, products, and information. Understanding these concepts is essential for effectively managing the overall supply chain.

Upstream operations refer to activities that occur earlier in the supply chain, closer to the source of raw materials or components. It involves the inflow of materials, information, and resources into the organisation. In other words, upstream activities focus on the processes involved in sourcing, procuring, and acquiring the necessary inputs for production.

For example, in the context of a manufacturing company, upstream operations would include activities such as sourcing raw materials, negotiating with suppliers, managing inventory levels, and coordinating transportation of goods from suppliers to the production facility. These operations are critical for ensuring a smooth and uninterrupted flow of materials into the organisation.

Conversely, downstream operations refer to activities that occur later in the supply chain, closer to the end customer. It involves the outflow of finished goods or products from the organisation to the market or end-users. Downstream activities primarily focus on the distribution, marketing, and delivery of products to customers.

For instance, in the same manufacturing company, downstream operations would involve activities such as packaging, warehousing, order fulfilment, distribution logistics, and customer service. These operations are crucial for delivering products to the right place, at the right time, and in the desired condition, meeting customer expectations and ensuring customer satisfaction.

The main distinction between upstream and downstream operations lies in the direction of material and information flow. Upstream operations deal with the sourcing and acquisition of inputs, while downstream operations handle the distribution and delivery of finished goods.

It's important to note that the differences between upstream and downstream operations may vary depending on the specific industry and context. For example, in the context of a food supply chain, upstream operations could refer to activities such as farming, harvesting, and processing, while downstream operations could encompass packaging, distribution, and retailing.

Benefits and Risks of Upstream SCM

Benefits of upstream SCM include reduced labour costs, lower inventories, increased sales due to better inventory management, enhanced control over product development, and a wider choice of suppliers. Risks may include technology integration challenges, organisational resistance to change, and the need for additional skills to operate new systems.

Benefits and Risks of Downstream SCM

Downstream SCM offers benefits such as product differentiation, two-way communication, better market research, easier online marketing, and customer-defined specifications. However, risks include supplier and distributor reactions, increased administrative costs, the risk of imitation, and a tendency to become reactive rather than proactive.

Effective utilisation of IT in SCM provides numerous advantages, including improved efficiency, enhanced coordination, better market responsiveness, and cost savings. However, organisations must also navigate potential risks and challenges associated with technology integration and organisational adaptation.

Big Data: Volume, Velocity, and Variety

Big data refers to the vast amount of data characterised by three main attributes: volume, velocity, and variety. The volume of data refers to the sheer amount of it available. Velocity indicates that data is generated rapidly, and variety highlights the diverse forms it can take.

Strategic Advantages of Big Data Exploitation

Leveraging big data offers several strategic advantages. Organisations gain a better understanding of their customers, allowing them to identify trends early and respond proactively. They can meet evolving customer needs, identify unsatisfied demands, conduct comprehensive market research, and enhance eMarketing efforts. Ultimately, exploiting big data provides a competitive advantage in the marketplace.

Disruptive Technology: FinTech

Disruptive technology refers to innovations that fundamentally change existing industry models. In the financial technology (FinTech) space, traditional banks such as HSBC and Barclays face disruption from online-based apps like Monzo, Revolut, Wise, and TransferWise. These digital banks offer advantages such as improved data utilisation, frictionless customer experiences, personalised products and services, cost-effectiveness without physical branches, and access to cheap capital. Disruptive technologies extend beyond FinTech and include examples like Uber, cryptocurrencies, and blockchains.

Defences Against FinTech Companies

Traditional banks can defend against FinTech companies by differentiating themselves, enhancing flexibility, promoting their physical presence, pursuing legal actions, targeting customers who prefer traditional banking, and developing their own disruptive technologies.

Cloud Technology: Advantages and Defences

Cloud technology, based on Internet connectivity, eliminates the need for local software and servers. Advantages of cloud technology include on-demand data sharing, self-service flexibility, collaboration capabilities (e.g., Dropbox, Google Drive), scalability, reduced maintenance, backup and disaster recovery options, and improved security. However, potential defences against cloud technology companies include reliance on providers, regulatory risks, data sharing concerns, and security vulnerabilities.

Unauthorised access to data is a significant concern, with instances of cloud-based data breaches making headlines. This brings us to artificial intelligence (AI), which is highly topical, with advancements such as Chat GPT. AI's link to unauthorised data access and its broader implications can be explored further.

Artificial Intelligence (AI) refers to a system's ability to accurately interpret external data and utilise the acquired knowledge to accomplish specific objectives. Through flexible adaptation, AI systems continuously learn from data and refine their processes to achieve desired outcomes.

Examples of AI include machine learning, supervised learning, unsupervised learning, and reinforcement learning. These are different approaches to AI, each with its own characteristics and applications.

Interlinking AI and Finance: Practical Examples

AI has significant applications in the field of finance. For instance, machine learning can be employed to automate accounting entries and enhance accuracy compared to rule-based methods. Platforms like Xero or Sage can automatically code transactions by learning from patterns and creating rules, streamlining processes for users.

AI can also enhance fraud detection by utilising sophisticated machine learning models, enabling financial institutions to predict and identify fraudulent activities more effectively. This has led to improved security measures, such as banks flagging suspicious transactions made in unfamiliar locations and contacting customers for verification.

Predictive models powered by machine learning enable revenue forecasting, leveraging historical data and patterns to anticipate future financial performance. Additionally, AI facilitates access to unstructured data, such as contracts and emails, enabling analysis and insights that were previously challenging to obtain.

Mobile Technology: A Transformative Force

Mobile technology, also known as smart technology, has revolutionised various aspects of modern life. This technology has caused major industries to undergo significant transformations, while new industries have emerged in its wake.

Impact on Industries

Industries such as newspapers have experienced a decline in physical sales due to the rise of online reading and targeted advertising. Platforms like Facebook provide smarter and more tailored advertisements to reach specific audiences. The music industry has shifted away from physical copies, with streaming services like Spotify and Apple Music dominating the market.

Banking is another industry greatly influenced by mobile technology, with a decline in traditional high street branches as digital banking platforms become more prevalent. Socialising has shifted to online platforms like Instagram and Facebook, altering the way people connect and communicate. Even the television and video industry has been transformed, with the rise of streaming platforms like Netflix and Amazon Prime.

Ethics and Legal Considerations in Technology Usage

In the UK, the General Data Protection Regulation (GDPR) plays a crucial role in governing the legal aspects of technology usage. Data controllers are required for each country, ensuring compliance with regulations when dealing with personal data.

Ethics and social considerations are vital in technology usage. Investor confidence relies on companies demonstrating ethical practices. Customers seek assurance and trust in the ethical use of technology. Ensuring customer safety is crucial to attracting and retaining employees and maintaining stakeholder confidence. Sustainability is another significant ethical and social consideration that affects business operations positively.

Incorporating ethical and social considerations brings various advantages to companies. It fosters trust and confidence among stakeholders, enhances reputation, and aligns business practices with societal expectations.

Corporate Digital Responsibility (CDR)

Corporate Digital Responsibility (CDR) is a novel concept that extends the principles of Corporate Social Responsibility (CSR) to the digital realm. Many modern businesses are adopting CDR strategies to address the ethical implications of their digital activities. There are five key areas a CDR strategy should cover:

1. **Digital Stewardship: Responsible and Secure Data Usage**

CDR emphasises the responsible and secure use of data, ensuring that organisations handle data ethically and with utmost security.

2. Meeting Customer Expectations: Transparency and Data Use

Customers increasingly expect transparency in how their data is used. CDR strategies aim to address these expectations and provide clear communication regarding data usage.

3. Giving Back to Society: Sharing Data and Collaborating

CDR encourages businesses to contribute to society by sharing valuable data, such as clinical trial data with university researchers. By doing so, companies demonstrate their commitment to social responsibility.

4. Recognising Data Value: Importance of Ethical Data Practices

Data value is increasingly recognised by both customers and businesses. CDR strategies highlight the significance of ethical data practices to ensure the responsible and beneficial use of data.

5. Digital Inclusion: Accessibility and Support

CDR promotes digital inclusion by proactively supporting users who may face barriers or obstacles in accessing technology. This includes addressing issues faced by individuals with visual impairments or disabilities, making digital content and platforms more accessible.

E-Businesses: Types, Benefits and Risks

Information technology plays a vital role in the strategic planning process. It assists in strategic analysis by leveraging business strengths and overcoming weaknesses. From a strategic choice perspective, it can create a competitive advantage and provide access to new markets. When it comes to strategic implementation, information technology facilitates business process improvement and should be considered at every stage of the syllabus.

Impact of Information Systems on Industries (Porter's View)

According to Porter (2008)[8] information systems or technology can affect industries in three ways:

1. **Creating New Businesses:** Examples include auction sites and photo album sites, which have replaced traditional physical methods with online platforms.
2. **Changing Industry Structure:** The music business is an example where online platforms have disrupted the traditional model. Artists can now publish their own music, sell it online, and even stream it, bypassing the need for physical stores and publishers.
3. **Providing Competitive Advantage:** Organisations can gain a competitive edge by leveraging information systems and technology to operate more efficiently. For instance, airlines save costs by encouraging online bookings instead of relying solely on customer service consultants.

Types of E-Businesses

E-businesses can be categorised based on the delivery and exchange initiator:

- Business to Business (B2B): Transactions between businesses.
- Business to Consumer (B2C): Transactions between businesses and consumers. Examples include Amazon and other online retailers.

---

[8] *Porter, M. E. (1980). Competitive Strategy: Techniques for Analyzing Industries and Competitors. New York : Free Press ; Toronto : Maxwell Macmillan Canada.*

- Consumer to Business (C2B): Consumers offering products or services to businesses.
- Consumer to Consumer (C2C): Consumers engaging in transactions with other consumers, as seen on platforms like eBay.

Stages of E-Business

The four stages of e-business development are:

1. Web Presence: Creating a website to establish an online presence.
2. E-commerce: Selling products or services online.
3. Integrated E-commerce Website: Developing an integrated e-commerce website with Enterprise Resource Planning (ERP) integration, combining various business processes.
4. Fully Fledged E-Business: Reaching a stage where the organisation operates as a comprehensive e-business entity.

Benefits of e-businesses include cost reduction, increased efficiency, revenue growth, improved information for control, enhanced visibility, better customer service, marketing improvements, automation, and competitive advantage. However, barriers such as technophobia, security concerns, setup and running costs, limited business opportunities, and resource constraints can pose challenges for e-businesses.

Risks and Controls in Information Technology

Risks associated with information technology include unauthorised access (hacking), viruses or malware, hardware failure or loss, and input errors. To mitigate these risks, controls can be implemented:

- **General Controls**: Logical access controls, physical controls, and backups.
- **Application Controls**: Output checking and reasonable checks.
- **Software Controls**: Diligent software supplier selection, unique licensing codes, and one-time codes.
- **Network Controls**: Firewalls, data encryption, and virus protection.
- **Cybersecurity**: Developing a written policy, providing training and assessments, dedicating cybersecurity staff, limiting data volume, and automating systems.

Chapter 16 - Online Marketing

Online marketing is also referred to as eMarketing. We will explore the concept of the marketing mix, commonly referred to as the seven P's. Additionally, we will discuss eBranding, online branding, and how marketing strategies are applied in e-businesses.

The Marketing Mix: The Seven P's

Traditional marketing involves finding the right combination of elements, commonly known as the four P's: price, promotion, product, and place. However, eMarketing expands this concept by adding three more areas: people, physical evidence, and processes.

When considering an online marketing company or a company looking to expand online, the focus should be on the traditional four P's while giving more attention to the following areas:

1. Price
Determining the right pricing strategy for online products and services is crucial. Online businesses often face intense competition, and pricing plays a significant role in attracting customers. For example, an e-book publisher might offer special discounts or bundle deals to entice customers to purchase multiple titles.

2. Promotion
Developing effective promotional tactics is essential to reach and engage the target audience online. Online platforms provide various avenues for promotion, such as social media advertising, influencer collaborations, email marketing, and search engine optimisation. For instance, a fitness app can run targeted Facebook ads, partnering with fitness influencers to endorse its features and benefits.

3. Product

Creating compelling and marketable products or services suited for the online platform is vital. Online businesses must consider factors such as digital delivery, scalability, and user experience. For example, a software-as-a-service (SaaS) company might offer a free trial of its product, allowing users to experience its functionality before making a purchasing decision.

4. Place

Optimising the online presence by strategically selecting distribution channels and platforms is key. Online businesses can leverage e-commerce platforms like Amazon, eBay, or their own website to reach a wider audience. They can also explore partnerships with online marketplaces that cater to specific niches. For instance, a handmade jewellery brand might list its products on a marketplace dedicated to supporting independent creators like Etsy.com.

5. People

The people element emphasises the importance of having well-trained staff involved in the online marketing process. These individuals play a crucial role in executing marketing strategies, managing customer interactions, and maintaining the online presence of the business. For example, a skilled social media manager can effectively engage with customers, respond to queries, and promote the brand on various social media platforms.

6. Physical Evidence

Physical evidence includes elements such as websites, which serve as a form of tangible proof of a company's online presence. A well-designed and user-friendly website acts as a digital storefront, providing customers with information about products or services, showcasing testimonials, and displaying visual content like images or videos. For instance, a clothing brand's website can feature high-resolution images of its products, allowing customers to view them from different angles and make informed purchasing decisions.

7. Processes

Processes refer to the procedures and methods employed in online marketing. It encompasses various aspects, such as order processing, customer service, supply chain management, and fulfilment. Streamlining these processes is essential to ensure a seamless customer experience. For example, an e-commerce business may implement automated order fulfilment and shipment tracking systems to provide customers with real-time updates on their purchases.

Combining the traditional marketing mix with the additional three elements results in the comprehensive framework known as the seven P's of online marketing.

The Six I's: Differentiating New Media from Traditional Media

The six I's serve as differentiating factors between new media (online) and traditional media (such as TV, print, etc.). Let's explore each of these in more detail:

1. Interactivity

Interactivity distinguishes the push approach of traditional media from the targeted pull approach of online advertising. Traditional media, like television, broadcasts ads to a wide audience, whereas online platforms allow for personalised advertisements based on user preferences. For example, a streaming service might recommend TV shows or movies to users based on their viewing history.

2. Integration

Integration refers to the balance between online advertising and physical store presence. It involves seamlessly integrating online advertising efforts with offline operations and considering the impact of both channels on the overall marketing strategy. An example of integration is when a retail brand promotes exclusive online discounts through social media while simultaneously advertising in-store sales events.

3. Intelligence

Intelligence relates to the data collection capabilities of websites and online platforms. Online marketing provides opportunities for businesses to gather valuable customer insights through analytics tools, website tracking, and user behaviour analysis. For instance, an e-commerce store can analyse data to identify popular products, track conversion rates, and optimise marketing campaigns based on customer preferences.

4. Individualisation

Individualisation highlights the personalised nature of online advertising facilitated by tracking users' online behaviour through cookies. This targeted approach contrasts with the mass communication of traditional media, which may not be relevant to all recipients. For example, an online bookstore can display personalised book recommendations based on a customer's browsing and purchase history.

5. Industry Structure

Industry structure explores the efficiency of supply channels and the potential to eliminate intermediaries and reduce the need for physical store employees. Online businesses can operate with fewer personnel compared to brick-and-mortar stores, leading to cost savings and increased revenue. For instance, a direct-to-consumer clothing brand can streamline its operations by eliminating the need for physical retail locations, reducing overhead costs, and offering competitive pricing to customers.

6. Independence of Location

Independence of location emphasises the global accessibility of online businesses. Unlike physical stores limited to specific locations, online businesses can reach customers worldwide through the World Wide Web. This opens up new market opportunities and allows businesses to cater to diverse customer segments. For example, an online language learning platform can provide language courses to students around the globe, breaking down geographical barriers.

Understanding the marketing mix and the six I's is crucial for effective online marketing strategies. By considering these elements, businesses can leverage the unique opportunities offered by the online platform to connect with their target audience, increase brand visibility, and drive business growth. Whether it's optimising the online presence, personalising advertisements, or leveraging data-driven insights, online marketing opens up a world of possibilities for businesses to thrive in the digital landscape.

E-Branding

E-branding, also commonly referred to as online branding is somewhat different to traditional branding. This chapter will provide real-life examples to illustrate these key differences and similarities.

When it comes to e-branding, businesses can adopt various strategies to establish and promote their online presence. Let's examine these strategies in more detail:

1. Matching an Existing Brand

Matching an existing brand involves extending an established brand's identity and values into the online realm. This strategy capitalises on the existing brand's reputation and recognition, providing a seamless experience for customers across different channels. For example, a clothing retailer with a strong offline presence might create an online store that mirrors its physical stores in terms of branding, product offerings, and customer experience.

2.   Modifying an Existing Brand

Modifying an existing brand entail adapting it to suit the unique demands of the online environment. This may involve refining the visual identity, messaging, or user experience to cater to online preferences and behaviours. A classic example is when a traditional publishing house rebrands itself and creates an e-book platform to cater to the growing digital reading market. The modified brand maintains its core identity while embracing digital innovations.

3.   Creating a New Brand

Creating a new brand tailored explicitly for the online platform allows businesses to start from scratch, considering the distinct characteristics and requirements of the digital landscape. An example is the online streaming service Netflix, which began as a DVD rental-by-mail company. Recognising the shift in consumer behaviour, they rebranded as a streaming service, focusing solely on online content delivery. This new brand successfully tapped into the burgeoning demand for digital entertainment.

4.   Forming Partnerships with Existing Brands

Collaborating with an existing brand can be a strategic move to enhance your online presence. Partnering with a complementary brand helps leverage each other's strengths and target a wider audience. A prime example is the partnership between Spotify and Uber. Users could stream their favourite music during their Uber rides through the Spotify app, offering an integrated and enjoyable experience for both companies' customers.

E-Branding vs. Traditional Branding

E-branding possesses distinct characteristics that set it apart from traditional branding. Let's examine these differences and provide examples to illustrate each aspect:

1. Efficient Information Delivery

In the online environment, information needs to be conveyed quickly and efficiently to capture users' attention. E-branding focuses on concise and compelling messaging that can be easily consumed in a digital context. An excellent example of efficient information delivery is Twitter, with its limitation of 280 characters per tweet. Brands effectively utilise this platform to share concise messages, announcements, and promotions, ensuring they grab users' attention in a brief span of time.

2. Visual Identity Importance

Online branding places greater emphasis on visual identity due to the highly visual nature of digital platforms. Engaging visuals, such as well-designed websites, eye-catching graphics, and captivating videos, play a crucial role in capturing and retaining online users' interest. An example is Apple's website, which combines sleek design, stunning visuals, and intuitive navigation to create a visually appealing and immersive online experience that reflects the brand's premium image.

3. Ease of Accessibility

Online branding requires ease of access and navigation to ensure a seamless user experience. Websites should be user-friendly, with clear menus, intuitive interfaces, and responsive designs that adapt to different devices. Airbnb exemplifies this aspect by providing a user-friendly website and mobile app that allow users to easily search for accommodations, view property details, and make bookings, regardless of the device they use.

4. Interactivity

One of the advantages of e-branding is the ability to offer interactive experiences to engage users. Interactive elements like quizzes, games, and personalised recommendations create a sense of active participation and personal connection. The shoe company Nike, for instance, utilises interactive design elements on its website, such as a shoe customisation tool and interactive training programs, to provide users with engaging and personalised experiences that go beyond passive browsing.

5.   Evolutionary Nature

Online branding offers the flexibility to adapt and evolve more rapidly compared to traditional branding. Digital platforms allow brands to make quick adjustments, test new strategies, and gather real-time data to refine their online presence. An example is Coca-Cola, which embraces online trends and social media platforms to launch digital marketing campaigns that evolve in response to user feedback and emerging trends, keeping their brand relevant and engaging.

Using Marketing in an Online Business

When operating an online business, effective marketing strategies are crucial for acquiring and retaining customers. Here are some key approaches to consider:

Search Engine Marketing (SEM)

Search Engine Marketing involves optimising your website's visibility on search engines to drive organic traffic and attract potential customers. Search Engine Optimisation (SEO) is a fundamental aspect of SEM, focusing on improving your website's ranking in search engine results. For example, a website designer operating in all London (UK) boroughs might optimise their website to appear higher in search results when users search for keywords like "website designers Chelsea." This increased visibility can lead to higher website traffic and conversions. Some companies nowadays even name their brand with the keywords they wish to rank for, for example take   'www.WebsiteDesigners.London' (also shortened to 'www.WDL.digital' to make searching even easier for potential clients).

Pay-Per-Click Advertising (PPC)

Pay-Per-Click advertising allows businesses to place ads on search engine result pages and other online platforms, paying only when users click on their ads. Google Ads is a popular PPC platform where businesses bid on keywords to display their ads to relevant audiences. For instance, a travel agency might create a PPC campaign targeting keywords like "best vacation packages" to attract users actively searching for travel options.

Social Media Marketing

With the widespread popularity of social media platforms, businesses can leverage them to connect with their target audience and promote their products or services. Platforms like Facebook, Instagram, Twitter, and LinkedIn provide opportunities to engage with potential customers through content, paid advertising, and influencer partnerships. For example, a skincare brand might run an Instagram advertising campaign showcasing their products and their benefits to target audiences interested in skincare and beauty.

Online PR and Content Marketing

Online PR involves using digital platforms to distribute press releases, expert blog posts, and other forms of content to generate brand awareness and attract media attention. Content marketing, on the other hand, focuses on creating valuable and relevant content to engage and educate potential customers. By publishing informative blog articles, videos, or podcasts, businesses can position themselves as industry experts and build trust with their audience. An example is a software company that publishes blog posts about the latest industry trends and offers practical tips for optimising software usage, thereby establishing credibility and attracting potential customers.

Online Partnerships and Affiliates

Collaborating with other online businesses and influencers through partnerships and affiliate programs can significantly expand your reach and customer base. This strategy involves mutually beneficial relationships where partners promote each other's products or services to their respective audiences. For instance, a fitness equipment brand might partner with a fitness influencer who promotes their products on social media, reaching a targeted audience interested in fitness and exercise.

Email Marketing

Email marketing remains a powerful tool for nurturing customer relationships and driving conversions. By building an email subscriber list, businesses can send targeted and personalised messages to their audience, such as promotional offers, newsletters, or product updates. For example, an e-commerce store might send personalised emails to customers who abandoned their shopping carts, offering discounts or incentives to encourage them to complete their purchase.

Utilising various online marketing strategies, such as search engine marketing, social media marketing, content marketing, and email marketing, allows businesses to effectively reach and engage with their target audience in the digital landscape. By leveraging the power of digital platforms, businesses can expand their online presence, attract new customers, and build long-term relationships, ultimately driving growth and success in the online business sphere.

E-branding strategies encompass matching, modifying, creating, and partnering with brands to establish a strong online presence. Online branding differs from traditional branding by focusing on efficient information delivery, visual identity, accessibility, interactivity, and adaptability. By understanding and harnessing the unique aspects of online branding, businesses can effectively engage their target audience, build brand loyalty, and thrive in the digital landscape.

Chapter 17 - Project Management

We'll explore the essential components of project management, including the project lifecycle, business case documents, risk analysis, project planning and initiation, key project staff, and project controls and reviews.

A project is an endeavour that has a defined beginning, middle, and end. It involves the allocation and utilisation of resources to achieve specific objectives. Let's examine the project lifecycle, which outlines the various stages a project goes through.

1. **Initiation**: The project begins with the initiation phase, where the need for the project is established. This involves constructing a business case or a business plan to justify the project's purpose and potential benefits.
2. **Planning**: Once the project is approved, the planning stage begins. During this phase, detailed plans are created, outlining the project's scope, objectives, timelines, and resource requirements. This stage sets the foundation for the execution of the project.
3. **Execution**: The execution phase involves implementing the project plan. It is during this stage that project activities are carried out, and resources are allocated accordingly. Effective controls are established to monitor progress and mitigate risks.
4. **Control**: Project controls play a crucial role in ensuring that the project stays on track. This involves monitoring performance against established targets and measures, making adjustments as necessary, and taking proactive actions to address any deviations.
5. **Completion**: The final stage of the project is completion, where the project's objectives are achieved, and the deliverables are finalised. This

stage often involves transitioning the project outputs into regular business operations or handover to the client.

The Importance of Business Case Documents

A business case document is a formal document that justifies the need for the project and outlines its potential benefits. It serves several purposes, including:

- **Strategic Analysis**: It provides a strategic analysis of how the project aligns with the organisation's goals and objectives.
- **Project Benefits and Costs**: It outlines the anticipated benefits and costs associated with the project, helping stakeholders assess its viability.
- **Project Constraints**: It identifies the constraints and limitations that may impact the project's execution, such as time, budget, or resource constraints.
- **Project Risks**: It identifies and assesses potential risks and uncertainties that may affect the project's success, allowing for proactive risk management strategies.

Analysing and Mitigating Risks

Risk analysis is a critical aspect of project management. It involves three stages: risk identification, risk assessment, and risk mitigation. By evaluating the likelihood and impact of risks, appropriate actions can be taken. Here are common risk response strategies:

- **Avoidance**: High likelihood and high impact risks are best avoided by eliminating or changing project aspects that give rise to the risk.

- **Acceptance**: Risks with low likelihood and low impact may be accepted without active mitigation efforts, but they should still be monitored.
- **Transfer**: Risks with high impact but low likelihood can be transferred to external parties, such as insurance companies or subcontractors.
- **Reduction**: Risks with high likelihood but low impact can be reduced through proactive measures, such as implementing additional controls or safety measures.

Crafting a Project Plan

A project plan provides a roadmap for executing the project effectively. Key stages in developing a project plan include:

1. **Resource Understanding**: It is crucial to determine the resources required for the project, including time, budget, and personnel.
2. **Detailed Schedule**: Creating a detailed schedule, often represented through tools like Gantt charts, helps visualise the project timeline and milestones.
3. **Targeted Measures**: Defining specific targets and performance measures allows for clear evaluation and monitoring of project progress.
4. **Communication and Monitoring**: Effective communication and continuous monitoring are essential throughout the project to ensure alignment and address any issues promptly.
5. **Exit Plan**: As the project nears completion, an exit plan outlines how the project will transition into regular business operations or conclude effectively.

Key Project Staff

Successful project management involves collaboration among various key staff members. Here are the primary roles:

- **Project Sponsor**: The project sponsor, usually a senior-level individual, provides oversight, resources, and approves changes. They communicate organisational goals and support the project's success.
- **Project Manager**: The project manager is responsible for overseeing the project, ensuring that team members are on track, executing the project plan, and managing project controls.
- **Team Members**: Team members are involved in executing the project's operational tasks, following the project plan, and enabling the desired change.

Project Controls and Reviews

To maintain project performance and address deviations, effective controls and reviews are necessary. Here are some essential aspects:

- **Performance Measures and Targets**: Establishing specific, measurable, achievable, relevant, and time-bound (SMART) performance measures and targets helps evaluate progress and success.
- **Milestone Testing**: Conducting performance tests at relevant project milestones or gateways allows for the identification of any deviations from the project plan.
- **Control Actions**: If performance measures and targets are not being met, control actions can be taken. These may include fast-tracking, adding resources, reducing project scope, or ensuring high employee motivation.
- **Project Review**: The post-project review (PPR) assesses team performance, while the post-implementation review (PIR) evaluates the project's outcomes and success.

By following these project control practices and conducting thorough reviews, organisations can enhance project performance and achieve desired outcomes.

Project management is a crucial discipline for successfully executing projects. By understanding the project lifecycle, creating comprehensive business case documents, analysing and mitigating risks, developing effective project plans, involving key project staff, implementing control measures, and conducting reviews, businesses can increase their chances of project success. These project management practices contribute to efficient resource allocation, timely delivery, and the achievement of project objectives.

Chapter 18 - Financial Decision Making

This chapter focuses on financial decision making, which is a popular topic amongst growing start-ups, specifically the topic of how to secure funding for a business. We will discuss various aspects such as raising finance, breakeven analysis, marginal decision making, budgeting, dealing with risk and decision making, and other quantitative techniques.

Options for Raising Finance

Raising Finance: Equity and Debt

When it comes to raising finance, there are two primary avenues to consider: equity and debt. Understanding the nuances of each is essential for determining the best approach for your business.

Equity Options

- **Internal Equity: Retained Cash and Working Capital**
  Utilising retained cash or working capital, which your business has generated and accumulated over time, can be a less risky option. It allows you to tap into your own resources to fund your operations.
- **External Equity: Existing Shareholders and Issuing New Shares**
  External equity involves seeking additional investment from existing shareholders or issuing new shares. While this approach can inject capital into your business, it carries the risk of diluting the value of existing shares and may involve engaging with the stock market, friends and family, or crowdfunding platforms.

Debt Options

- **Long-Term Debt: Debentures and Mortgages**

Long-term debt options include debentures, which are debts secured against specific assets, and mortgages, typically associated with property financing. These provide a stable source of funding but involve commitments and repayment obligations over an extended period.

- **Medium-Term Debt: Leasing and Bank Loans**
  Leasing arrangements, similar to renting, can be a viable medium-term debt option for acquiring necessary assets. Alternatively, obtaining a bank loan can provide the required capital with defined repayment terms.
- **Short-Term Debt: Overdrafts and Extended Payables**
  Short-term debt options include utilising an overdraft facility, allowing you to temporarily exceed your account balance, or extending payment terms with suppliers to manage cash flow effectively.

Other Sources of Finance

In addition to equity and debt, exploring alternative sources of finance can expand your funding options. Consider the following possibilities:

- **Government Grants**: Governmental bodies often provide grants to support businesses involved in specific sectors or projects. Exploring these opportunities can provide much-needed financial assistance.
- **Venture Capitalists and Business Angels**: Venture capitalists and business angels are individuals or firms that invest in promising business ventures in exchange for equity or a share in the business. They can provide not only funding but also valuable expertise and guidance.
- **Selling Spare Assets**: If your business possesses unused or surplus assets, selling them can generate additional funds to support your operations.

Factors to Consider in Choosing a Source of Finance

Selecting the right source of finance requires careful consideration of several factors:

- **Cost**: Evaluate the expenses associated with the chosen finance option, such as interest rates, fees, or equity dilution.
- **Availability**: Assess the feasibility and accessibility of the finance option, considering factors like eligibility criteria or the willingness of investors or lenders to provide funds.
- **Control**: Consider the level of control you can retain over your business with each finance option, as some sources may come with conditions or influence in decision-making.
- **Cash Flow**: Analyse how the chosen option will impact your cash flow. Assess whether the repayment terms align with your revenue streams and business cycles to ensure sustainable operations.
- **Security**: Examine the security arrangements associated with the chosen finance option. For debt financing, this includes collateral or guarantees that may be required.
- **Gearing**: Understand the impact on your business's level of indebtedness, as this can affect your overall financial stability and risk profile.
- **Exit Routes**: Plan for repayment or exit strategies associated with the chosen finance option, particularly in the case of debt. Ensure that you have a clear plan in place to settle the borrowed funds when the time comes.

By carefully evaluating these factors, you can make an informed decision about the most suitable source of finance for your business. This will not only address your immediate funding needs but also contribute to the long-term financial health and stability of your venture.

Financial decision making is a complex process that requires a deep understanding of various options and factors. By exploring the different avenues for raising finance, considering alternative sources, and evaluating the key factors in choosing a source of finance, you can navigate the world of funding with confidence. Armed with this knowledge, you will be well-equipped to make sound financial decisions that propel your business forward and support its growth and success.

Cost Accounting

Cost accounting allows you to examine the expenses involved in maintaining the current business model. It primarily focuses on the total cost of production in manufacturing, considering both variable costs and fixed costs. Cost accounting relies on standard costing systems, as well as absorption, marginal, or activity-based systems. However, it has become increasingly outdated in modern manufacturing environments. Nevertheless, key areas in cost accounting include breakeven analysis, appraisal, decision making, risk and uncertainty, budgeting, and various forms of analysis.

Understanding Breakeven Analysis

Breakeven analysis is concerned with determining the amount of revenue required to cover costs. The formula for calculating the breakeven point is dividing the total fixed costs (independent of business activity) by the contribution per unit, which is the sales minus variable costs. The breakeven revenue can be calculated by dividing the total fixed costs by the contribution margin. It's important to note that variable costs are costs that fluctuate in proportion to the level of business sales.

Exploring the Margin of Safety

The margin of safety is determined by subtracting the breakeven sales from the budgeted sales. It represents the cushion a business has in terms of sales above the breakeven point.

Breakeven analysis has certain limitations. It assumes a constant selling price, disregards economies of scale or diseconomies of scale, struggles to accommodate stepped or changing fixed costs, and is only applicable in the short term.

Marginal Decision Making

Marginal decision making involves analysing variable costs and revenues that are relevant to specific decisions. It is particularly useful in accepting or rejecting special orders, closing a business unit, or abandoning a project. When using marginal decision making, costs and revenues must meet three criteria: they should consider future costs and revenues, incremental costs and revenues, and the overall impact of the decision.

When employing marginal decision making, it's essential to factor in opportunity costs, which involve the potential gains from using the allocated funds elsewhere. Additionally, the accounting and tax impacts of the decision may differ.

Introduction to Investment Appraisal

Investment appraisal involves evaluating the suitability of various investment options. Four commonly used methods in investment appraisal are net present value (NPV), payback period, accounting rate of return, and internal rate of return (IRR).

Net Present Value (NPV)

NPV utilises the cost of capital and discount factors to determine the present value of future cash flows. It provides an estimate of the impact on shareholder wealth. It is advantageous in situations where the project is long-term and the cost of capital is known. Nevertheless, it relies on a reliable cost of capital estimate.

Payback Period

The payback period indicates how quickly the initial cash injection is recovered. It is useful when the project is short-term and there is limited cash availability. The payback period provides a minimum target for project life. However, it requires a benchmark for comparison.

Accounting Rate of Return (ARR)

The accounting rate of return is calculated by dividing the average profits by the initial investment. It is best used when a product has specific performance targets. The advantages include simplicity and reliance on readily available information. However, it can be easily manipulated.

Internal Rate of Return (IRR)

The internal rate of return determines the cost of capital that results in a zero net present value. It assesses the profitability of a projected or potential investment. IRR is useful for long-term projects where the cost of capital has not been determined. It reveals the highest acceptable cost of capital. However, it is not suitable for comparing projects.

In reality it is good practice to not to rely on one of these forms of analysis, instead a combination of these investment appraisal techniques is recommended when assessing potential investments.

When it comes to decision making and managing risk, there are several approaches to consider. Let's explore these approaches with some examples.

Expected Value Calculation

Calculating the expected value involves summarising all possible outcomes by calculating a simple weighted average. For instance, let's say you're considering launching a new product. You estimate that there's a 40% chance of the product being highly successful and generating £100,000 in profits, and a 60% chance of it performing moderately and generating £50,000 in profits. The expected value calculation would be: (40% * £100,000) + (60% * £50,000) = £70,000. This expected value represents the long-term average profit you can anticipate.

Decision Trees

Decision trees are a visual representation of complicated scenarios. Let's consider an example in the context of expanding a business. The decision tree could start with the question, "Should we open a new branch?" If the answer is "Yes," the tree branches out with further questions such as "Is the location favourable?" and "Do we have sufficient funds?" Depending on the answers, the decision tree leads to specific outcomes, such as "Open a new branch," or "Postpone expansion plans." Decision trees help analyse complex decision paths and consider various factors influencing the final decision.

Budgeting

Budgeting plays a crucial role in managing finances effectively, whether it's personal finance or organisational budgeting. Let's explore some practices that can enhance the budgeting process.

Serious Attitude to Budgets

For example, if you create a budget for personal expenses, you should have a serious attitude towards sticking to it. This means consciously making choices that align with your budgeted amounts for different categories like groceries, entertainment, or transportation.

Managerial Buy-In

In an organisational setting, managers must buy into the budget and actively support the budget targets. For instance, a marketing manager needs to understand and work within the allocated budget for advertising and promotions to ensure effective resource allocation and achieve desired outcomes.

Data Analysis and Reporting

When managing a budget, it's essential to have established data sources and analyse and report on budget results. For instance, a business may regularly analyse sales figures and compare them to the budgeted sales to determine whether they are meeting their revenue targets. Timely reporting and analysis allow for corrective actions to be taken if deviations from the budget are identified.

Variance Analysis

Variance analysis involves comparing actual results to the budgeted figures and investigating the reasons behind any deviations. For example, if a department's expenses exceeded the budgeted amount, a variance analysis can help determine the causes, such as unexpected price increases or higher-than-planned utilisation of resources. This analysis enables appropriate actions to be taken, such as implementing cost-saving measures or adjusting future budgets.

Quantitative Analysis Techniques

In addition to variance analysis, quantitative analysis techniques can provide valuable insights. Let's consider an example in the context of sales forecasting. By using linear regression analysis, historical sales data can be analysed to predict future sales based on factors like advertising expenditure, market size, or previous sales trends. This quantitative technique helps make informed decisions about resource allocation, production planning, and revenue projections.

These techniques, such as linear regression, correlation analysis, and time series analysis, offer valuable quantitative analysis tools. These tools can enhance your decision-making abilities and enable you to incorporate data-driven insights into your budgeting process.

Chapter 19 - Managing Change

In this chapter, we will discuss managing change, specifically strategic change. We will cover the types of change, the influence of culture on change, preparing for change, change management styles, the Change Kaleidoscope developed by Hailey, V. H., & Balogun, J. (2002)[9], and the POPIT Model, as a framework for effective change coordination which was popularised by the International Institute of Business Analysis (IIBA) as part of their Business Analysis Body of Knowledge (BABOK).

Types of Change

There are four main types of change to consider: transformational change, realignment change, big bang change and incremental change.

Firstly, let's examine the severity and extent of change. How big and drastic is the change?

1. **Transformational Change:** This involves changing the culture of an organisation. It is a significant and comprehensive change. For example, a company decides to shift from a traditional hierarchical structure to a more collaborative and flat organisational structure. This change impacts the entire organisation and its way of operating. For example, let's consider a company that undergoes a transformational change. Imagine a traditional manufacturing company that decides to shift its focus towards sustainability and eco-friendly practices. This change would involve a significant

---

[9] Hailey, V. H., & Balogun, J. (2002). Devising Context Sensitive Approaches To Change: The Example of Glaxo Wellcome. Long Range Planning, 35(2), 153-178.

cultural shift, impacting the organisation's values, processes, and even product offerings.

2. **Realignment Change**: In this type of change, the assumptions and beliefs of an organisation remain the same. It is a less drastic change compared to transformational change. For instance, a company decides to reorganise its departments and streamline its processes while keeping the existing organisational culture intact.

Additionally, we need to consider the scope of change.

3. **Big Bang Change:** This refers to a drastic and immediate change. It can be used in transformational change, such as rapidly changing the culture—a revolution. For example, a company might undergo a complete rebranding and restructuring, including changing its core values, mission statement, and visual identity, all at once.

4. **Incremental Change:** This involves making small, gradual changes. Evolutionary change is an incremental transformational change that occurs gradually through interrelated activities or initiatives. It is more proactive and requires the participation of future changes. An example of incremental change is when a company introduces new technology systems in different phases, gradually replacing outdated systems over time.

On the other hand, if we consider incremental change from a realignment perspective, where the assumptions and beliefs of the organisation remain the same, it is known as adaptation. Adaptation entails realigning the organisation's operations through a series of steps. For instance, a company might implement new customer service protocols and communication tools to improve efficiency and meet changing market demands while maintaining its existing organisational culture.

Lastly, if we have a realignment change implemented through the big bang approach, it is called reconstruction. This type of change aims to realign the organisation's operations through multiple simultaneous initiatives. It is often forced and reactive due to changes in the competitive context. For example, a company facing intense competition may undergo a complete restructuring of its business units, product lines, and supply chain to remain competitive.

The types of change we have discussed are evolution, adaptation, revolution, and reconstruction. It is important to remember that we have two different extents of change—transformational and realignment—and two different scopes of change—big bang and incremental.

Influence of Culture

Culture plays a significant role in influencing change within an organisation. The Cultural Web developed by Johnson et al. (2009)[10] – a group of prominent management scholars and authors - provides insight into the routines and rituals that shape an organisation's culture.

Some factors that influence culture include:

- **Morning Meetings**: Regular morning meetings can help employees understand their tasks and contribute to the overall performance of the company. For example, a company may have a daily morning huddle where teams discuss goals, share updates, and align their efforts for the day.

---

[10] Johnson, G., Scholes, K., & Whittington, R. (2009). Exploring Corporate Strategy: Text & Cases. Pearson Education.

- **Organisational Structures**: The type of organisational structure, whether flat or hierarchical, can have a significant impact on the organisational culture. For instance, a company with a flat organisational structure encourages collaboration, open communication, and shared decision-making among employees, fostering a more egalitarian and innovative culture.

- **Power Structures**: The presence of autocratic or democratic managerial roles within an organisation affects its culture. An organisation with autocratic power structures may have a top-down decision-making approach, where managers hold most of the decision-making authority.

Let's consider a tech company known for its creative and innovative culture, like Google. Their cultural practices, such as open office spaces, flexible work hours, and a strong emphasis on employee well-being, contribute to a collaborative and innovative work environment.

Having a strong culture offers several advantages. It fosters effective communication, promotes a sense of belonging and social identity among employees, strengthens the organisation's values and attitudes, and influences the organisation's strategy and ability to adapt to change.

However, strong culture also has its disadvantages. It may create a negative perception among stakeholders, hinder organisational flexibility and adaptability, limit the organisation's capacity to learn new skills, and potentially prioritise inappropriate values or ethical concerns.

Preparing for Change: The Lewin's Three-Stage Model

Lewin's three-stage model provides a framework for preparing and implementing change. It consists of unfreezing, changing, and refreezing (Lewin, K. 1951)[11]. Unfreezing involves creating motivation for change by highlighting the drawbacks of the current culture. Changing entails implementing necessary changes to strategies, processes, and culture. Finally, refreezing involves reinforcing the new patterns of behaviour through recognition, rewards, and positive reinforcement.

Overcoming Resistance to Change: Change Management Styles

To address resistance to change, various change management styles can be employed. Six common approaches include encouraging participation, providing support and facilitation, manipulation (though somewhat unethical), negotiation, exercising power, and educating and communicating the reasons and benefits of the change.

The Change Kaleidoscope: A Comprehensive Model

The Change Kaleidoscope is a comprehensive model that provides organisations with a holistic framework for effective change management. It considers various contextual factors that influence the success of change initiatives. These factors include the time required for change, the scope of change, preservation of change, diversity of change, organisational capabilities, readiness for change, and power dynamics.

By taking these factors into account, organisations can make informed decisions and develop strategies that align with their specific change needs. The model emphasises the importance of understanding the time aspect of change, allowing organisations to allocate resources and set realistic timelines. It also highlights the need to consider the scope of change, whether it is incremental or transformational, to tailor strategies and resource allocation accordingly.

---

[11] Lewin, K. (1951). Field theory in social science: selected theoretical papers (Edited by Dorwin Cartwright.).

Furthermore, the Change Kaleidoscope underscores the significance of preserving change over time. Organisations must implement measures to reinforce and embed changes to prevent regression and ensure long-term sustainability. The model also recognises the diversity of change initiatives within organisations and the need to manage their interplay effectively.

Overall, the Change Kaleidoscope offers a comprehensive approach to change management, enabling organisations to navigate the complexities of change by considering key contextual factors. By applying this model, organisations can increase the likelihood of successful change implementation, foster a positive change culture, and achieve sustainable results.

The POPIT Model: Coordinating Change

The POPIT model, comprising People, Organisation, Process, and Information Technology, emphasises the importance of integrating these four factors within a business system. This model recognises that successful change can only be achieved when these elements work harmoniously together.

For example, let's imagine a manufacturing company implementing a new production system. The success of this change initiative depends on how well the people adapt to the new processes, how effectively the organisation supports and manages the change, and how the information technology infrastructure enables the new processes.

Managing change requires a deep understanding of its various dimensions. By recognising the different types of change, appreciating the influence of culture, adopting effective change management styles, and leveraging frameworks like the Change Kaleidoscope and the POPIT model, organisations can navigate change successfully and achieve desired outcomes.

Conclusion

Congratulations on making it to the end of this comprehensive guide—'Becoming A Strategic Business Leader: The Ultimate All-In-One Guide.' From the nuts and bolts of strategic planning to the nuances of governance, from the fundamentals of performance analysis to the imperatives of managing change, you've been through a transformative journey aimed at equipping you with the tools and knowledge you need to excel as a business leader in today's complex and dynamic environment.

In the first few chapters, you learned about the core principles behind strategic planning. With frameworks like Five Forces, Porter's Diamond, and SWOT Analysis, you're better equipped to analyse the strategic landscape. Performance analysis techniques and the Strategy Clock Model guide you towards crafting and refining your competitive edge.

Effective governance is non-negotiable in the corporate world. As we explored governance principles, agency theory, and approaches to governance, the importance of aligning organisational structures with strategic goals became apparent. The relationship between leadership and governance plays a pivotal role in your journey to becoming a strategic leader. Effective leaders are more than just decision-makers; they shape organisational culture and serve as ethical role models for their teams.

Stakeholder engagement and corporate social responsibility (CSR) aren't mere buzzwords—they are integral to long-term success. You've learned how to develop CSR strategies and understand stakeholder claims, ensuring that you operate not just for profit, but for the greater good.

Technology and digital transformations are shaping the future. Through chapters on Information Technology, Online

Marketing, and Big Data, you've gained insights into leveraging technology to stay ahead in the competition while being cautious of the ethical implications.

Project management and financial decision-making are quintessential skills. From crafting effective project plans to budgeting and investment appraisals, these chapters equipped you for making informed financial decisions vital for growth and sustainability.

Managing change is perhaps the ultimate test for a leader. By understanding the types of change and the influence of culture, you can navigate the treacherous waters of organisational transformation with greater skill and sensitivity.

As you close this book, remember that becoming a strategic business leader is not a destination but a continuous journey. The tools, strategies, and insights you've gained are your companions on this journey. The world of business is ever-changing, and the ability to adapt, learn, and grow is what will set you apart from the rest.

So, what's next? The answer is up to you. You're now armed with an all-in-one guide, but tools are only effective in the hands of those who know how to use them. Implement what you've learned, be mindful of the evolving business landscape, and never stop learning.

Thank you for letting this book be a part of your leadership journey. Here's to your continued growth and success as a strategic business leader of tomorrow.

Best wishes,
Adam Niazi

Acknowledgements

To my late grandfather, my namesake, Ahmed Niazi (1923-2021)

Dede, you've been one of my biggest cheerleaders.

I dedicate this book to your memory.

www.ingramcontent.com/pod-product-compliance
Lightning Source LLC
Chambersburg PA
CBHW071644210326
41597CB00017B/2110